Don't Panic—More Dinner's in the Freezer

Don't Panic— More Dinner's in the Freezer

A Second Helping of Tasty Meals You Can Make Ahead

Susie Martinez
Vanda Howell
Bonnie Garcia

Revell
Grand Rapids, Michigan

Published by Revell
a division of Baker Publishing Group
P.O. Box 6287, Grand Rapids, MI 49516-6287
www.revellbooks.com

Printed in the United States of America

Library of Congress Cataloging-in-Publication Data
Martinez, Susie.
Don't panic—more dinner's in the freezer : a second helping of tasty meals you can make ahead / Susie Martinez, Vanda Howell, and Bonnie Garcia.
p. cm.
Includes bibliographical references and index.
ISBN 978-0-8007-3317-9 (pbk.)
1. Make-ahead cookery. 2. Quick and easy cookery. 3. Cookery (Frozen foods) I. Howell, Vanda, II. Garcia, Bonnie. III. Title.
TX652.M29352 2009
641.5′55—dc22 2008049540

The recipe for the Orange Pine Nut Chicken pictured on the front cover is found on page 148.

12 13 14 15 16 9 8 7 6 5

Susie lovingly dedicates this book to her incredible husband and children, Joe, Chris, and Cassie: thank you for your love and your unending willingness to try new recipes. To my parents, thanks for the memories of years of freezing food at home. To Grandma Beutler, thank you for standing me on a chair in your kitchen in Wakarusa, Indiana, and teaching me to prepare my first meal—I never encounter a grilled cheese sandwich without thinking of you. To Dr. Saxby, your gift made my part of this book possible. To Vanda and Bonnie—the memories are priceless.

Vanda dedicates this book to her husband and son, Mike and Elliott. Thanks for being my rock, encourager, and comic relief. To my mom and dad, who gave my siblings and me the legacy of an open door for our friends at dinnertime: you always knew it was about more than just the food. To my two cookbook co-authors: you are my cohorts, my partners in cooking crime, but most importantly, when it gets down to where the rubber meets the road, you are my dear friends who have become my family. It has been an adventure that I would never trade.

Bonnie would like to dedicate this latest book to her awesome family: to my best friend, Steve, and my incredible boys Nate, Daniel, and Johnny. You guys have cheered me on in this project. I could not have done it without your constant support, honest feedback, and enthusiasm for trying new meals! Thanks to my mom, Shirley Burke, who taught me how to cook. I will never forget sitting up on the kitchen counter as a little girl, making brownies from the Betty Crocker cookbook! Thanks to Vanda and Susie for being my true friends with whom I can always be myself.

Most importantly, we collectively thank God for bringing this concept and these books "that never were intended to be books" into being. We are all better for being able to see how God used our insignificant voices to impact thousands of families' lives with the simple concept of having more time for what is truly important.

Contents

Preface

When someone at Revell referred to our first cookbook as "the little cookbook that could," we thought there was no better way to sum it up. *Don't Panic—Dinner's in the Freezer* has been a book that people buy because someone they know loves it and uses it endlessly. It is not a book that became popular, had its moment in the spotlight, and then faded away. It continues to chug along, as we hear from people all over the world who own it.

When asked to write a second book, we wondered if we would be able to build a new collection of freezable treasures as good as the first. However, after months of feeding our brave families and friends new recipes, we proudly present you with a book that, in our estimation, is even better than the first. When we went to the mountains to edit this book, we got hungry just thinking about making these dishes again. As with the first Don't Panic collection, we think you will like any recipe you try. So go ahead and get started . . . and feel free to let us know what you think. We always love hearing from you. Enjoy!

Acknowledgments

Thank you to so many of our dear friends and readers for your input, comments, and support over the years. To those of you who contributed to this book through proofreading, taste-testing, and recipe submissions, we thank you. Although we were unable to include every recipe that was submitted, we appreciate all of the input that we received. We would like to acknowledge the following people, whose recipes were included in the book. In our opinion these recipes are real "winners"!!

Jan Barreth
Suzanne Berg
Terri Bisio
Shirley Burke
Joanne Decker
Beth Doll
Beverly Garrison
Tami Hastings
Flo Kitashima
Cassie Martinez
Kaye Matthews
Donna Mayberry
Paula McGuire
Peggy McMillen
Jenny Mills
Leslie Reisig
Mary Sares
Wes Scheu
Karen Schultz
Amy Sunahara
Marla White
Bev Wirtz
Cher Zall
Pam Zundel

We would like to thank our editor, Lonnie Hull DuPont, for her patience in bringing this project together. Thank you for hanging in there with us and believing in Don't Panic number two!!

Introduction

It was the funniest thing, I thought, when Bonnie's three-year-old son climbed up on a chair one cooking day to inspect three large stockpots of cooled chili sitting on the counter. They were the fruit of our labors, trophies—the products of blood, sweat, and tears. Beautiful to behold! And in the blink of an eye this little guy, with a hand as quick as lightning, pulled a stockpot of chili off the counter and onto the floor. You should have seen it! It was as if a volcano had erupted into the air, with tiny red droplets of tomato sauce landing on cupboards, light fixtures—and the neighbor's roof.

It was funnier yet, I thought, when Bonnie knelt down to scoop up all the chili not directly touching the floor and return it to the pot to be packaged for the freezer. Desperate times call for desperate measures!

If you ask a roomful of people to raise their hand if they feel they have a lot of free time each day, few would do so. Instead of enjoying an elegant *dinner* with *wine*, most moms would say their kids *whine* while they *dine*. If you ask a single professional how many home-cooked meals they eat, many would laugh and say they know a local waiter by name. My retired parents are representative of a group who has "been there and done that" with the world of cooking. They recently discovered, with excitement, that the grocery store deli makes mashed potatoes—a little thick and pasty, but edible.

Cooking every day is a pain. Few have the time, patience, or desire to do so. The question of what to have for dinner haunts people from all walks of life. The question begins in the morning, and by the end of daylight hours, it demands an answer.

So who wrote this book? Who are we? We are a nurse, a kitchen designer, and a therapist. We cook together, but we also laugh and cry together. For me, personally, Vanda and Bonnie have become the sisters I never had. And it all started years ago with three young women looking for friendship, fellowship, and an easier way to get dinner to their families. Are you thinking about trying it? What do you have to lose? Grab a friend or two and embark on this journey. You will find you share much more than meals together. The rewards will catch you by surprise.

It took us years to tell Bonnie's husband the "chili on the floor" story, but perhaps we didn't wait quite long enough. He mentioned something about needing to trust the person who cooks your food, and we realized it might have been best to keep this incident just between us. So a word of caution: if something completely hysterical happens when cooking with your friends, try to determine if "you had to be there" to see the humor in it.

Get excited! This is going to be fun!

Susie

Cooking the Don't Panic Way

This book is your guide for preparing healthy, great-tasting meals available at a moment's notice. We hope it becomes an invaluable tool for you in your own cooking. Its design lets you prepare multiple meals with minimal effort, which means you will spend less time, money, and energy cooking better meals than ever. The recipes in this book have been freezer-tested and refined—and most of all, they are the ones our own families like! We have learned a lot as we have cooked together over the years, and we are happy to pass these tips on to our readers. Here are five practical steps that will be helpful in making the Don't Panic method of cooking easy to implement.

Step One: Get Started

The Don't Panic cooking method can be implemented simply by choosing your favorite family recipe and doubling or tripling it. For example, if you are making lasagna, triple the recipe, have one for dinner that evening, and then put the other two meals in the freezer to serve at a later time. In its simplest form, making recipes in quantity is what the Don't Panic method is all about.

Step Two: Choose a Day

Preplanned activities that actually make it to the calendar tend to be the ones that get done. Practically speaking, this step requires looking at your daily and weekly responsibilities and choosing a block of time out of the week for cooking. Even designating a two- to three-hour block of time for cooking is usually enough to make six to nine meals! This may involve a weekday morning or afternoon if you are home during the day; it may be in the evening or on the weekend if you work full time outside the home.

Step Three: Check Weekly Loss Leaders

The term *loss leaders* refers to items that supermarkets sell below cost to entice you to shop at their store. The other full-price items you buy while shopping make up for the loss the store takes on loss leaders.

Supermarkets usually rotate their loss leaders on a weekly basis. Stores will promote these items through weekly advertisements distributed in a local newspaper, through the mail, or online. To track loss leaders, you will need to consistently consult weekly supermarket ads. You will soon know when these ads are distributed and how long a supermarket sale is effective. As you do this regularly, it becomes easier to recognize and take advantage of great loss leaders.

To illustrate how you can save big by shopping loss leaders, consider this example, which uses Grilled Coconut Lime Chicken Tenders as the Don't Panic entrée. If you are cooking with two friends, you will need approximately fifteen pounds of boneless chicken. If boneless chicken is a loss leader in a local supermarket, it will be advertised at around $1.99 per pound. That's $29.85 for fifteen pounds of chicken. On the other hand, if the chicken was purchased at the regular price of $4.99 per pound, you would have spent $74.85. By simply shopping loss leaders and planning your cooking menu accordingly, you have just saved $45.00 on the meat item alone! By doing this consistently, you will never pay full price for your entrées.

Another important way to make the Don't Panic cooking method economically beneficial is to custom package according to what your family will actually eat rather than according to the directions in the recipe. Custom packaging is described in detail in "Wrapping It Up" on page 21. By simply shopping loss leaders and custom packaging by family size, your savings can be incredible! Each entrée included in this book should average between $5.50–$7.50 to feed a family of four. Please note that this cost is per family, not per person.

Step Four: Choose Your Recipes for Cooking Day

After checking local ads to determine weekly loss leaders, choose one or two recipes for cooking day that use those discounted items. For example, if flank steak is on sale, choose entrées that use flank steak on cooking day (Asian Flank Steak and Steak Soft Tacos, for example). The key is to avoid paying full price for meat items. Cook according to what is on sale!

Occasionally there will be a week when you cannot use a loss leader to cook entrées. During those weeks, you can still avoid paying full price for meat items by having a baking day instead. Choose from your favorite muffins, rolls, breads, pizza dough, cookies, or desserts. These items freeze very well if you follow appropriate packaging instructions. See the instructions for freezing baked goods on page 24.

Step Five: Construct Your Shopping List

Your shopping list should be made before going to the grocery store. By using the quantity tables found in this book, you can accurately determine the amount of each ingredient you will need for each recipe. For example, if you are cooking by yourself and tripling the recipe, refer to the "x3" column for correct quantities. If you are cooking with two other people and are each tripling the recipe, refer to the "x9" column. For more grocery shopping tips, see the next chapter, "Hitting the Market."

Hitting the Market

Tips on Shopping

As we have cooked together over the years, we have come across some shopping tips that will be very helpful as you begin the Don't Panic cooking method.

One: Know the Value of Warehouse Stores

One question we are frequently asked is, "What about shopping at warehouse stores?" We have found that warehouse stores (Sam's Club and Costco, for example) are great for certain large quantity items such as cooking oil, flour, sugar, nuts, and cheese. Also available in large quantity are freezing supplies such as freezer bags, disposable gloves, wider-width aluminum foil, and plastic wrap. These items will be significantly lower in price at warehouse stores than at the grocery store, even if you're using coupons.

If the cost of an annual membership is a concern, consider sharing a membership with your cooking partners. One person can buy the membership and you can split the cost between you. Warehouse stores usually allow a member to bring in guests when shopping.

One note: We have found that supermarket sales still offer the greatest savings on most meats if you shop the loss leaders.

Two: Invest in a Community Box

If you regularly cook with other people, invest in a community box. You can use this box to store bulk-quantity items that are regularly used on cooking day. The items you keep in your community box might include freezer bags, foil, plastic wrap, vegetable oil, spices, flour, sugar, and salt. Buy these items in large quantity and divide the cost among the members of your cooking team. Although you may pay more initially, in the long run it is worth the investment!

Three: Get to Know Your Butcher

When you are cooking with large quantities of meat, you can save time by asking your supermarket butcher to prepare it for you. For example, if you're making

Chuck Roast for the Grill, have your butcher run the roast through a tenderizing machine. If you are making Shish-Ka-Bobs, ask your butcher to cube the meat. You'll be surprised what your butcher will do for you!

Having your meat prepared ahead of time will save you hours on cooking day! Most stores offer this service as a courtesy at no extra charge. Just be sure to give your butcher some extra time. Call ahead and place your order, or have your butcher prepare your meat while you shop.

Four: Shop the Day before Cooking

It's best to do your shopping the day before your cooking day. This will allow you to make the most of your time on cooking day. If cooking with friends, it usually works best to have one person shop for the whole group. Just bring your receipts, divide the costs, and reimburse the shopper.

Now you're ready to start cooking!

Stirring the Pot

Hints for Cooking Day

Here are some helpful hints for cooking day.

One: Organizing Your Groceries

On cooking day, assemble all groceries and ingredients necessary for the recipes you'll be preparing. If you are cooking with others, check the community box (see "Invest in a Community Box" on page 16) for any of the bulk items needed for cooking or packaging.

Two: Preparing Your Ingredients

Read through your recipes to determine what items need to be prepared. If you're cooking with others, divvy up! Assign each person a task. To make cleanup easier, keep a sink full of soapy water available. When you're finished with a pan or utensil, let it soak while you're completing the recipe.

Chop all the vegetables first

If you're preparing two different entrées on cooking day, refer to both recipes to see what steps can be combined in food preparation. For example, if both dishes call for chopped onions, chop all of the onions you need for both. Then set aside the appropriate quantity of onions for each recipe.

Prepare the meat or poultry

If the meat or poultry item you're using needs to be cut up or browned, do that next. You may want to have your butcher cut your meat for you. See "Get to Know Your Butcher" on page 16.

Measure out any liquid or dry ingredients needed

To save time and effort, refer to the equivalency chart in the back of this book when measuring larger quantities of ingredients. For example, if you need 12 teaspoons of an ingredient when doubling or tripling a recipe, refer to the chart and measure out 4 tablespoons or ¼ cup instead.

Three: Following the Recipe as Written

Begin to assemble all the prepared ingredients according to the recipe's directions. If you're doubling or tripling a recipe, be prepared by having two or three separate mixing bowls or pans to accommodate the larger quantities of ingredients. Also see "Customizing Your Cooking" below.

Four: Cooling Food

When applicable, let the prepared food cool and come to room temperature. Doing so will help prevent the ice crystals that are likely to form if a meal is packaged and sealed while it is still hot or warm. To speed the cooling process, place potholders on the shelves in your refrigerator, then place the warm food on the potholders. Be sure the hot pans do not touch anything else in your refrigerator. When the food is cool, package it according to your family size. See "Wrapping It Up" on page 21.

Five: Finishing Up

We use the "cool down" time to clean up, eat lunch, feed the kids, and calculate our grocery receipts for reimbursing the shopper. Then we custom package our meals and return home with a lot of great meals and wonderful feelings of accomplishment and success.

Six: Trying New Recipes

On your cooking day, in addition to the meals you plan to prepare and freeze, try one new recipe for dinner that night (using the same "loss leader" item you're cooking with that day). If it's a keeper, add it to your repertoire of recipes. You might consider preparing a very small portion to see how it freezes. Be sure to make notes to yourself so you can change, correct, or customize the recipe according to your family's likes and dislikes.

Seven: Customizing Your Cooking

"I couldn't sneak a chopped onion or green pepper past my family no matter how deeply I buried them in the dish!" Don't let picky eaters or food allergies discourage you. Custom cooking lets you adapt your meals according to your family's likes and dislikes by simply adding or omitting ingredients in a particular recipe.

If cooking with a friend, you can accommodate family preferences by designating a separate pan on the stove for each family. This allows each of you to customize the recipe according to your family's tastes and needs.

Eight: Keeping Baked Goods Moist

- *Muffins*: When baking, you might consider slightly under-baking muffins so they are almost done but not doughy. Muffins should be only slightly browned on top. This will ensure a moist, fresh-baked taste when they are reheated.
- *Breads/Quick Breads*: Breads and quick breads should be completely baked. Be careful not to over-bake, to ensure the bread stays moist.
- *Quiches*: Bake quiches just until a knife inserted in the center comes out clean. This keeps the quiche from drying out when reheated on serving day.

Wrapping It Up

How-tos for Packaging and Freezing

As you consider using the Don't Panic method of cooking, one obstacle you may face is the lack of a separate freezer in which to store large quantities of food. We encourage you to begin working with the space that you have available. By incorporating some of our custom packaging and freezing hints, you will be able to store quite a few meals in your refrigerator's freezer alone. As our cooking method becomes more a part of your lifestyle, you may want to invest in a chest or upright freezer. This will allow you to prepare larger quantities of meals, as well as take better advantage of sale items at your local grocery store.

One: Custom Packaging

An essential component of the economic savings of the Don't Panic method is to package meals according to your family size. On cooking day, after you have prepared your recipes and are ready to put them into the freezer, package your meals according to how much your family will eat at each meal.

For example, if you are preparing Chicken Enchiladas with a yield of eight enchiladas per recipe, tripling the recipe will provide three casserole dishes of eight enchiladas each. This is a total of twenty-four enchiladas. If your family eats only six enchiladas for dinner, the recipe can be divided into packages of six enchiladas each. You have now made four meals instead of three! This stretches your loss leader savings even more.

Two: A Word about Containers

In choosing containers in which to freeze our meals, we have found that high quality freezer bags (not storage bags) work well in most cases. As a general rule, plastic containers take up too much space in your freezer and should be passed up for better space-saving techniques. Recently, makers of plastic storage products have developed more freezer-friendly containers that are smaller in size. If you find a serving size container that works well for your particular freezing needs—use it. Otherwise, consider the freezing methods described below.

Three: Flash Freezing

This term refers to the method of putting an item in the freezer for a short period of time in order to quick-freeze it into a particular shape. Once the food item reaches a solid state, it is removed from the "molding" or shaping container and then returned to the freezer for long-term storage; this is described in more detail in the packaging section that follows.

Four: Methods of Freezing

A. Freezer Bag Method

- *When to use it*:

  Liquid: Use this method when freezing items such as soup, chili, and stew.

  Semisolid Food Items: Use this method when freezing items that DO NOT need to hold a particular form, such as meats in marinade, stroganoff, and barbecue shredded beef.
- *How to do it*: When using the freezer bag method, place your meal in the freezer bag, remove as much air as possible, and seal. Then take a cake pan, or another pan with sides, and lay the bags flat, stacking one on top of the other in the pan. The cake pan will not only freeze the meals flat, giving you more freezer room, but will also help ensure that any leaks will be kept within the pan. Place the pan in the freezer. Once the items have been flash frozen (see "Flash Freezing" above), remove them from the pan and stack the bags inside your freezer. Meals that are frozen flat thaw much more quickly than meals put in the freezer in a random clump.
- *On serving day*: When defrosting, make sure you place the item in the refrigerator with a pan, plate, or bowl underneath to catch the extra moisture (or leaks) from defrosting. For your health and safe food handling, we do not recommend defrosting the meal on the kitchen countertop, as this promotes the growth of harmful bacteria. If you need to speed up the defrosting process, consider using the defrost cycle on your microwave oven. (See "Reaping the Rewards" on page 26.)

B. Foil and Plastic Wrap Method

- *When to use it*: semisolid food items. Use this method when freezing items that DO need to hold a particular form, such as Smothered Breakfast Burritos, Mediterranean Lasagna, and Black Bean Tortilla Bake.

- *How to do it*: When using the foil and plastic wrap method, line a baking dish first with aluminum foil and then with a layer of plastic wrap (make sure that the foil and plastic wrap are large enough to cover the bottom, sides, and top of the dish). If your food is hot, allow it to cool slightly. Fill the dish with your prepared meal. When completely cool, seal the plastic wrap, removing as much air as possible. Then seal the outer aluminum foil layer. With the wrapped and sealed meal still in the pan, place it in the freezer. Once the item has been flash frozen, slip the meal out of the pan and into a freezer bag. (See "Flash Freezing" on page 22.)
- *On serving day*: Remove the meal from the freezer. Remove foil and plastic wrap, then place the meal back in its original dish for baking. If you have a little trouble getting the plastic wrap off, place the meal in the microwave for 30 to 60 seconds on the defrost setting or quickly dip it in warm water. The plastic wrap should then come off easily.

If you need to speed up the defrosting process, consider using the defrost cycle on your microwave oven. (See "Reaping the Rewards," page 26.)

- *Advantages of foil and plastic wrap method*:

  Baking dishes aren't tied up in the freezer.

  Pans are removed after the meals are frozen solid; the meals will stack compactly in the freezer.

  Your meal fits back into the original pan for thawing and baking or cooking.

C. Plastic Freezer Wrap Method (Alternative to Foil and Plastic Wrap Method)

With new products continuously entering the food storage market, there has been a recent development of a self-sealing plastic wrap that has an adhesive on one side. Because of how this wrap is made, it maintains the quality of frozen food and usually requires no additional freezer storage products to protect against freezer burn. Below are some tips to freeze meals utilizing this product, should you choose to use it.

- *When to use it*: semisolid food items. Use this method when freezing items that DO need to hold a particular form, such as Smothered Breakfast Burritos, Mediterranean Lasagna, and Black Bean Tortilla Bake.

- *How to do it*: When using the plastic freezer wrap method, line your baking dish, making sure that the wrap is large enough to cover the bottom, sides, and top of the dish. If the pan is wider than the freezer wrap, use two sheets and make a seam in the middle of your dish, so that the sheet is large enough to seal all edges. Press firmly on the seam with your finger to ensure a good bond. If your food is hot, allow it to cool completely. Fill the dish with your prepared meal. Seal the plastic freezer wrap, removing as much air as possible. Sealing is done by pressing the edges together, making seams along the top and sides of your dish. With the packaged meal still in the pan, place it in the freezer. Once the meal has been flash frozen, slip it out of the pan. Your meals may now be uniformly and efficiently stacked in the freezer. Be sure to date and label the meal.
- *On serving day*: Remove the meal from the freezer. Remove plastic freezer wrap, then place meal back in original dish for baking. If you have a little trouble getting the wrap off, place the meal in the microwave for 30 to 60 seconds on the defrost setting, or quickly dip it in warm water. The plastic freezer wrap should then come off easily.

D. Baked Goods

- To help ensure freshness and taste, we recommend double wrapping baked items. Wrap baked items in plastic wrap, then place in a freezer bag.
- *Cookies*: Cookie dough may be flash frozen by placing formed cookie dough balls on cookie sheets in the freezer for 10 to 20 minutes. Remove and place dough balls in freezer bags. Cookie dough for cutout cookies can be formed into disks (making for easier rolling) and then wrapped and sealed with plastic wrap and placed in freezer bags. For slice-and-bake cookies, form cookie dough into "logs" and wrap thoroughly with plastic wrap; seal the ends well and put into a freezer bag. Frozen cookie dough may go directly from freezer to cookie sheet for baking. Cookies may also be frozen after baking and double wrapped.
- *Muffins, rolls, and quick breads*: Freeze baked muffins, rolls, and quick breads by wrapping in plastic wrap and then placing inside a freezer bag. To give these items a "fresh-baked" taste, it is important to bake them just until done. Remove baked goods from the oven when they appear very lightly browned. Cool before wrapping. Package these items in serving size quantities (i.e., 6 muffins or 1 to 2 mini loaves).

- *On serving day*: Baked breads, muffins, or rolls can be brought to room temperature or defrosted in the microwave.

Five: Finishing Up

Date and label your meals—no one likes mystery meals! Also note specific cooking time and temperature, and any special recipe instructions. Items may be labeled by writing directly on the plastic freezer wrap or freezer bag with permanent marker. Freezer moisture will sometimes cause tape labels to fall off.

Reaping the Rewards

Suggestions for Thawing and Defrosting Your Meal

We recommend thawing/defrosting food either in the refrigerator or microwave, or by cold-water immersion. For *baked goods only* we suggest room temperature thawing. Depending on your time frame, each method works equally well.

Refrigerator Method

If you're organized enough to take out your meal ahead of time (or like some of us, finally remember), use this method. Allow at least 6 to 12 hours for refrigerator thawing, depending on the type of meal and the meal thickness.

Freezer bag meals containing items such as marinated meat are more tender and flavorful if defrosted over time in the refrigerator. The meat or ingredients have more time to marinate.

Microwave Method

Obviously, the microwave is the quickest method for defrosting—especially for those of us who are time challenged!

To speed up the defrosting process, place the food being defrosted in a microwave-safe container. On most microwaves, the defrost setting is approximately 30 percent power. Start out defrosting for approximately 5 to 10 minutes for whole meals and approximately 3 to 6 minutes for individual portions. Check and rotate food every 2 to 3 minutes, until meal comes to a slushy consistency. At this point, finish defrosting the dish in the refrigerator until it is time to prepare your meal.

Cold Water Immersion Method

This method should only be used for meals that were frozen and sealed using the freezer bag method. Do *not* use this method for meals frozen with the foil and plastic wrap method.

For this method, place the freezer bag in a large bowl that will allow for the meal to be completely immersed. Make sure to check the freezer bag seal before immersing. Use very cold water, changing the water every 30 to 35 minutes, and allow the food to come to a slushy consistency. Discontinue this method after 2 hours. Don't use hot water, as it causes inconsistent thawing and may even start to "cook" the outside edges or layers of food.

Room Temperature Thawing—For Baked Goods Only

To thaw cookies, breads, cakes, or muffins, unwrap frozen baked goods and set on a tray or wire cooling rack for 30 to 45 minutes, depending on the item. To keep baked goods from drying out, cover loosely with plastic wrap until completely defrosted. Then rewrap with plastic wrap and store in a freezer bag or air-tight container.

Knowing Your Limits

How Long Your Meal Will Keep in the Freezer

Your goal should be to have a constant rotation of meals going into and coming out of your freezer. By following the packaging directions given in this book, you will maximize the length of time your meals will taste fresh and remain free from freezer burn. In general, after meals have been in your freezer for more than 3 to 6 months, they begin to lose premium texture and flavor. Although these meals do not pose a health risk when eaten, they may not have the optimal quality they had when you first prepared them. The following chart provides general guidelines for optimal freezing times.

Meals

Meat and poultry, cooked, in sauces (e.g., Spicy Peanut Chicken, Beef Tacquitos)	5–6 months
Meat and poultry, uncooked, in sauces/marinades (e.g., Maui Grilled Chicken Sandwiches, Asian Flank Steak)	see Raw Meats
Pasta dishes	2–3 months
Side dishes	2–3 months
Spaghetti sauce, chili, soups, stews	5–6 months
Quiche or egg dishes	3 months

Raw Meats

Chicken		10 months
Fish		2–3 months
Ground beef		3 months
Pork chops, ribs		2–3 months
Roasts	beef	7–9 months
	pork	4–6 months

Steaks	beef	7–9 months
	pork	2–3 months
Turkey	parts	4–6 months
	whole	6 months

Baked Goods

Muffins	3 months
Pizza dough	5–6 months
Quick breads	2–3 months
Yeast breads/rolls	2–3 months

Desserts

Cakes	2–3 months
Cookies	3–4 months
Frozen desserts	1–2 months
Fruit pie or pie filling	6 months

Making Life Easier

As the three of us cook together, we try many new things to make our "cooking life" easier. Here are a few hints, techniques, or gadgets we personally love. We have also compiled a list of cooking tips we have discovered over the years. We hope they will spur you on to more fun-filled adventures with the Don't Panic cooking method. More tips are also scattered throughout the book with the recipes in which their use would be most helpful.

Authors' Tips and Techniques

Susie secretly wears **swim goggles** when she cuts onions (really!). She says it's the only trick that's worked to keep her eyes from tearing up and burning so badly.

Once a month Susie uses the **dough hook** on her KitchenAid mixer to make several pizza dough balls for their Sunday night ritual of homemade pizza (see Four Cheese White Pizza, page 215).

Susie loves the **grill basket** for her grill. For an easy side dish to any grilled entrée, she places fresh or frozen vegetables (see Grilled Vegetable Medley, page 237) in the grill basket and gives them a wonderful new flavor!

Bonnie uses a **freezer bag** (instead of a pastry bag) to fill manicotti or stuffed shells. Simply place the filling in the freezer bag, cut off a corner, and squeeze the filling into the pasta tubes. No hassle, no mess, no cleanup. Just throw the freezer bag away! Also use this for quick-filling our Twice Baked Potatoes (see page 247).

Bonnie loves her **garlic press**! Many main dish recipes list garlic as an ingredient. A garlic press allows you to mince the garlic finely without getting it all over your hands. Throw it in the dishwasher when you are done for easy cleanup. Bonnie's favorite appliance is her **KitchenAid mixer**. One of her favorite things to do with it is to make cookies with her kids. There have been lots of memories shared in Bonnie's kitchen around that mixer.

The one item Vanda can't live without is **disposable latex gloves**. They work great for handling raw meat, chicken, fish, or doing any messy cooking job. You don't have to worry about contaminating everything you touch (like the phone, the faucet, or your kids). Just toss them in the trash when the phone rings and put on a new pair when you return to cooking! These gloves can be purchased in larger quantities at warehouse club stores.

Vanda's new favorite gadget is silicone, heat-resistant **basting brushes**. They come in a variety of fun colors and sizes. She uses them for drizzling oil into a pan, basting baked items, and oiling the charcoal grill. When you are done using these brushes, just throw them in the dishwasher. No more sticky oil or BBQ sauce stuck in the bristles!

The one kitchen appliance Vanda can't live without is her **food processor**. It shreds, slices, dices, purées, and even mixes pie dough in one minute or less—who could ask for more? She makes homemade salsa every week by dumping all the ingredients in at the same time—and in four pulses she has instant happiness.

Fun Facts for Fabulous Freezing

Vegetables

- Onions: Chop or dice onions and place ½ to 1 cup portions into small storage bags, then place inside a larger freezer bag. Date, label, and freeze. They will be ready to use when you need them.
- Ginger: Fresh ginger grates easily when frozen, and keeps a long time. Wrap in plastic wrap and place inside a small freezer bag. Label and freeze.
- Garlic: Store peeled cloves in a tightly sealed jar of olive oil. The oil can later be used for salad dressing. When fresh garlic is needed, take out a clove and mince or press.
- Blanching: Drop vegetables or fruit, such as tomatoes or peaches, in boiling water for a very brief time to loosen skins. Blanching can also be used to "par-boil" or pre-cook vegetables before freezing. After blanching, immediately plunge vegetables/fruit into ice cold water. This will stop the cooking process and set the color.
- Freeze leftover tomato paste in 1 tablespoon portions. Wrap each portion in a small piece of plastic wrap, sealing the edges, or in small storage bags. Drop them into a labeled quart-size freezer bag and store in the freezer. When you need tomato paste, it's always available!

Fruits

- Lemon, orange, or lime juice—Three methods to get more juice from any citrus fruit: (1) roll the fruit under your palm on a flat surface, pressing into the fruit as you roll. Cut fruit, and then juice; (2) place the fruit in a microwave oven for 30 seconds, cut in half and juice; or (3) immerse the fruit in a pan of boiling water for 30 seconds, cut in half and juice.
- Lemon, orange, or lime juice—If you have leftover lemons or limes, don't let them go to waste. Squeeze the juice into ice cube trays, or place 1 tablespoon portions in small baggies. Flash freeze the portions, and drop them into a labeled small freezer bag to store in the freezer.
- Lemons, oranges, and limes—After squeezing juice, store and freeze the leftover rinds in a freezer bag. When a recipe calls for fresh peel (see Orange Pine Nut Chicken, page 148), simply grate the frozen rind. This provides a fresh citrus taste without having to keep fruit on hand. Label and date before freezing.
- Making orange, lemon, or lime zest is much easier with a rasp grater. The rasp takes off only the bright, outer peel, which contains the essential oils that you want, without the bitter white peel. You can easily find these graters in kitchen stores. They are also available in hardware stores—they were originally used to shave off very thin pieces of wood!
- Fruit ripening tip: If your fruit is not ripe enough to use, place the fruit in a paper bag along with an apple, and close bag loosely. The fruit will be ready in a day or two. The apple produces a gas that speeds up the ripening process.
- Discoloration: To keep fruits and vegetables from turning brown, sprinkle with lemon juice or douse with a solution of lemon juice and water. Products like Fruit Fresh or ascorbic acid also work well.

Baking

- Eggs: Fresh eggs sink in water, stale eggs float; cooked eggs spin evenly, raw eggs wobble.
- Butter: Softened or room temperature butter is used a lot in baking. To quickly soften, place the butter (with the wrapper on) in a microwave-safe plate or shallow dish. Microwave the butter on medium-high using 5-second intervals, until softened. Watch very carefully. The butter is ready

when you can easily make an indentation in the top of the butter and it still holds its shape.

- For flakier pastry or pie crust: Use cold butter, margarine, or shortening.
- Measuring flour: Spoon the flour into a dry measuring cup and level off with a table knife or straight edge, rather than just "scooping" out a cup of flour. Never "tap down" flour (or white sugar) when leveling—it can make your baked goods taste too heavy or dry. Precise measurement will bring you the best results with baked goods.
- To make uniform size cookie dough balls: Use a small ice cream scoop or melon baller. If cookies start to stick, dip the scoop into a little flour.
- Baking powder: Replace it often! (Nothing's worse than having your favorite cake or brownies fail to rise.) Heat can sometimes make baking powder less effective. To test for freshness, mix 1 teaspoon of baking powder in a cup of hot water. It will bubble furiously if it is still active.
- Melting chocolate: Melt chocolate in a double boiler over barely simmering water. You can also use a tempered glass or metal bowl placed over a saucepan. For the microwave, place chocolate in bowl and cook on medium high (80 to 90 percent) power in 30-second intervals. Stir and check constantly.

Phyllo, Puff Pastry Sheets, and Wonton or Egg Roll Wrappers

Phyllo tips

If phyllo dough is frozen, for best results thaw in refrigerator for 24 hours, then leave dough at room temperature for two hours.

- When working with phyllo, cover sheets with plastic wrap to keep them from drying out. Place a damp kitchen towel over the plastic wrap on top of the excess phyllo sheets, working with one sheet at a time.
- Instead of brushing the sheets with butter, spray the phyllo with olive or canola oil for non-dessert recipes. For dessert recipes, spray sheets with imitation butter spray.

Puff pastry tips

Thaw puff pastry sheets at room temperature for 40 minutes before using. If you only need one sheet, wrap remaining frozen sheets in plastic wrap or foil and return to freezer. Note: when working with puff pastry, it is fine to thaw the pastry, prepare your meal, and refreeze. The quality of your meal will not be compromised.

Wonton or egg roll wrappers

These aren't just for making egg rolls! Use them in place of pasta for appetizers (see Quick Cheese Ravioli, page 221). Work with only a couple of wrappers at a time, keeping the rest covered with a damp towel.

Herbs and Nuts

- To substitute dried herbs for fresh: Use ½ to 1 teaspoon of dried, crushed, or powdered herbs for 1 tablespoon of fresh herbs.
- Leftover fresh herbs: Wrap in plastic wrap, then place in a labeled freezer bag and freeze. When needed, add directly to recipe.
- Toasting nuts: Toasting nuts brings out their flavor and intensity. In a preheated 350 degree oven, place the nuts in a baking pan and toast until golden brown. Stir occasionally. For stove-top toasting, place the nuts in a heavy pan over medium heat and toast for 5 to 10 minutes, stirring often. Watch closely to avoid burning. Immediately remove nuts from pan and allow to cool, as the nuts will continue to cook. Store in airtight container.

Meat, Chicken, and Fish

- Want to freeze ahead for your next barbecue? Form hamburger into individual patties. Lay plastic wrap or waxed paper between the patties, and place inside a larger freezer bag. As your grill heats up, pull out only what you need!
- Freeze individually marinated chicken breasts in pint-size freezer bags or zip-type sandwich bags, and then place them inside a larger freezer bag.
- Use muffin tins or small loaf pans for making smaller main dish portions. Think about kid-size servings, an elderly neighbor, or a single serving for yourself. A dozen meat "muffins" need only about 15 to 25 minutes to bake in a 350 degree oven, instead of the normal baking time for meatloaf.
- Season, slow cook, and shred roasts when they are the loss leader item. Freeze 1 to 2 cup portions in freezer bags for quick soft tacos, burritos, or steak sandwiches.
- Pre-packaged frozen chicken: If you are preparing a marinated chicken dish for the freezer and are using frozen, pre-packaged chicken, do not

thaw the chicken. Simply place the desired number of frozen chicken pieces into the freezer bag, pour the marinade or sauce over the chicken, and place back in freezer. On serving day, allow the chicken to marinate as it thaws in the sauce. (See "Reaping the Rewards" on page 26.)

- To cut chicken breasts for stir-fry or skewers: first slice the chicken in half horizontally, then slice across the grain into strips of desired width.
- Fish: Some fresh fish is available year round, but other types, like halibut, are only available from March to October. If fish is to be frozen, make sure it is fresh and not "previously frozen." Refreezing a previously frozen fish results in a mushy or mealy texture. Ask your fishmonger if the fish is truly fresh.

General / Miscellaneous

- Reuse your freezer bags, when possible. Freezer bags previously used to store uncooked chicken/beef/pork or marinated meals should **not** be reused. Bags that were used for baked goods or as the outer, second-layer wrap can be used many times.
- Use disposable aluminum foil pans as extra forms for freezing. When taking a meal to a friend, deliver it in a disposable pan and there will be none of the hassle of getting your dish back.
- Microwave heating: If you double a microwave recipe, increase the cooking time by half. If you cut the recipe in half, reduce the cooking time by one third.

Deciphering the Code

A Key to Our Recipe Icons

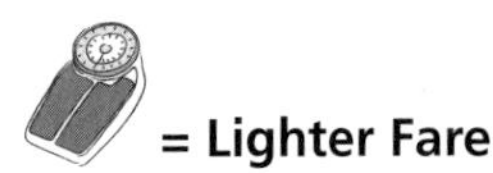

= Lighter Fare

These recipes are considered "lighter fare" because they are lower in total calories, total fat, or total carbohydrates—but they are not necessarily lower in all of these areas. The nutritional information listed on these recipes is approximate. If more precise measurements are needed, please consult a dietician.

= Crockpot

These recipes are suitable for cooking in the crockpot, and crockpot directions are included in the recipe instructions.

= Quick

These recipes are considered "quick" because their preparation time is 30 minutes or less.

= Entertaining

These are recipes that we personally serve to dinner guests. They may be more time consuming, but if so, they are worth the effort!

, , or = Authors' Top Three Picks

There are three recipes selected as a "top three pick" in each category—one favorite recipe from each author.

Mouthwatering Appetizers

Bacon Roll-ups

Goes over big with teens!

	x3	x6	x9
1 can crescent rolls	3	6	9
½ cup sour cream	1½c	3c	4½c
1 t. onion salt	1T	2T	3T
½ lb. bacon	1½ lbs	3 lbs	4½ lbs

Original Recipe Yield

24 appetizers

Cooking Day

Cook bacon until crisp. Place bacon on paper towels to drain, and then crumble. Stir onion salt into sour cream. Using a cookie sheet as a work surface, open and unroll can of crescent rolls. Cut each crescent roll into three triangles. Spread each triangle with sour cream mixture. Top each triangle with a generous amount of crumbled bacon. Beginning at large end, roll up each small triangle, curving the edges toward the center to form a mini-crescent. Place six rolled crescents on a piece of plastic wrap and seal. Freeze sealed packages, using freezer bag method.

Serving Day

Preheat oven to 350 degrees. Place rolled crescents on a lightly greased baking sheet (these can go directly from the freezer to the oven). Bake in oven for 8–10 minutes or until golden brown. Serve warm.

Beijing Egg Rolls

Take a day and make a bunch, it is worth the effort

Contributed by Cher Zall—Aurora, Colorado

	x2
4 whole heads garlic (8–10 cloves each)	8
1 small bag raw coleslaw, no dressing (approx. 4 cups)	2
6 bunches green onions	12
6 stalks celery	12
¾ lb. chicken, cooked and chopped	1½ lbs
8 oz. canned bamboo shoots, drained	16oz
8 oz. canned water chestnuts, drained	16oz
3 large carrots	6
½ lb. fresh bean sprouts	1 lb
½ cup peanut oil, divided	1c
1½ T. sugar	3T
2 T. peanut butter	¼c
2 T. soy sauce	¼c
64 egg roll wrappers	128
oil (for frying)	

Original Recipe Yield

64 egg rolls

Cooking Day

Chop the first 9 ingredients VERY fine and place each item in a separate bowl. (Do not use a food processor, as this will make ingredients too mushy!)

Stir-fry ingredients in batches, until crisp tender, as directed: In 2 T. peanut oil, stir-fry garlic and coleslaw together and drain. Using same pan, in 2 T. peanut oil stir-fry green onion, celery, and sugar; drain and set aside. In same pan, in

2 T. peanut oil, stir-fry chicken, bamboo shoots, water chestnuts, and peanut butter; drain and set aside. In 2 T. peanut oil, stir-fry carrots, bean sprouts, and soy sauce; drain and set aside. Mix all ingredients together in a large bowl and drain off any extra liquid. Place ¼ cup egg roll filling in center of each egg roll wrapper and wrap according to package directions. Package bundles of 4–6 egg rolls in plastic wrap, then place in freezer bags. Freeze using freezer bag method.

Serving Day

Thaw egg rolls completely. Fry egg rolls in oil in electric skillet or frying pan until golden brown. Serve with sweet and sour sauce or hot mustard.

Bleu Cheese Pine Nut Tart

A beautiful appetizer or first course!

	x2	x4	x6
Pastry shell			
1½ cups all-purpose flour	3c	6c	9c
½ t. salt	1t	2t	1T
½ cup butter, cold	1c	2c	3c
4–6 T. ice cold water	½–¾c	1–1½c	1½–2¼c
Filling			
8 oz. package cream cheese, softened	16oz	32oz	48oz
⅓ cup bleu cheese, crumbled	⅔c	1⅓c	2c
1–2 cloves garlic, minced	2–4	4–8	6–12
¼ cup heavy whipping cream	½c	1c	1½c
1 egg, slightly beaten	2	4	6
¼ t. cayenne red pepper	½t	1t	1½t
¼ t. coarse ground black pepper	½t	1t	1½t
⅓ cup roasted red bell pepper (from a jar), chopped	⅔c	1⅓c	2c
3 T. lightly toasted pine nuts (or your favorite nuts, toasted and chopped)	¼c + 2T	¾c	1c + 2T
2 T. fresh parsley, chopped	¼c	½c	¾c

Original Recipe Yield

14–16 servings; one 9–10 inch tart/pie pan or two smaller 6–7 inch tart/pie pans

Cooking Day

Preheat oven to 375 degrees.

Pastry: We recommend that you prepare the dough in small batches—no more than x2, even if you're preparing multiple tarts. Mix flour and salt together in a large mixing bowl; cut in butter with a pastry blender or fork until mixture resembles coarse crumbs. Stir in just enough cold water with fork, one tablespoon at a time, until the flour mixture is just moistened. The pastry may also be mixed in a food processor. Shape into a ball.

Roll out pastry on lightly floured surface into a 12 inch circle (if using two small pans, divide dough in half and roll into two 8 inch circles). Place in ungreased pie pan or tart pan with removable bottom. Press the dough firmly onto bottom and sides of pan. Cut away any excess pastry. Prick pastry all over with a fork—this will help keep it from "shrinking" in size. Bake for 17–22 minutes (15–20 minutes for small pans) or until very lightly browned. Cool.

Filling: In a large mixing bowl, combine cream cheese, bleu cheese, and garlic. Beat at medium speed until creamy. Scrape down the sides of bowl and continue to beat, gradually adding whipping cream, egg, cayenne pepper, and black pepper. Spread the mixture into the baked pastry shell and sprinkle with roasted red pepper, pine nuts, and parsley.

Freeze, using foil and plastic wrap method, making sure that the plastic touches the top surface of the tart.

Serving Day

Thaw tart slightly. Bake in a preheated 375 degree oven for 20–25 minutes, or until filling has set and a knife inserted in the middle comes out clean. Let stand 20 minutes before serving. To serve, cut into appetizer-size wedges. Carefully take tart out of pan and place on serving platter. (Cover and refrigerate any leftover pieces.)

Cocktail Meatballs with a Twist

Wonderful for a party or as a main dish served over rice or mashed potatoes

	x2	x4	x6
2 lbs. lean ground round or sirloin	4 lbs	8 lbs	12 lbs
1 t. salt	2t	1T + 1t	2T
¼ t. pepper	½t	1t	1½t
½ cup breadcrumbs	1c	2c	3c
½ cup chopped onion	1c	2c	3c
1 clove garlic, minced	2	4	6
2 eggs, beaten	4	8	12
1–10 oz. jar grape jelly	2	4	6
1–12 oz. bottle chili sauce (found in ketchup aisle)	2	4	6
juice of 1 lemon (2–3 T.)*	1½	3	4½

*This measurement, when multiplied, has been adjusted to accommodate the intensified flavor of acidic ingredients when recipes are made in quantity.

Original Recipe Yield

48 meatballs

Cooking Day

Combine ground beef, salt, pepper, breadcrumbs, onion, garlic, and eggs and form into balls about the size of walnut shells. Arrange meatballs side by side in an oblong baking dish. In a saucepan, mix together jelly, chili sauce, and lemon juice and simmer for 5 minutes, stirring occasionally.

Pour sauce over meatballs and bake at 325 degrees for 1 hour, basting 3 times during baking time.

If freezing meatballs for later use, cut baking time to 45 minutes. (Meatballs may not be totally cooked, but when reheated they will finish cooking and remain tender.) Cool completely. To freeze, place desired amount of meatballs along with some sauce into freezer bags. Freeze using freezer bag method.

Serving Day

Thaw meatballs and sauce. Over very low heat in saucepan, gently reheat meatballs and sauce, but do not boil. Meatballs may also be placed in oven-proof dish and reheated at 300–325 degrees until just heated through.

If serving meatballs as a main dish, serve over rice or mashed potatoes.

Hint

Use disposable gloves when making meatballs—it makes handling and cleanup a lot easier.

Crab Cheese Wontons

These disappear quickly in the Garcia house!

Contributed by Wes Scheu—Denver, Colorado

	x3	x6	x9
16 oz. cream cheese, softened	48oz	96oz	144oz
2 finely chopped green onions	6	12	18
6 oz. minced crab, or imitation crab, drained	18oz	36oz	54oz
1 t. salt	1T	2T	3T
4 t. grated parmesan cheese	¼c	½c	¾c
1 t. garlic powder	1T	2T	3T
1 t. ground ginger	1T	2T	3T
46 wonton wrappers	138	276	414
oil (for cooking)			

Original Recipe Yield

46 wontons

Cooking Day

Mix together cream cheese, green onions, crab, salt, parmesan cheese, garlic powder, and ginger until smooth. Put a small teaspoon of crab mixture on wonton. Moisten the edges of wonton with a little water and fold into a triangle—or press centers of each edge together to form a flower shape. Cook in a "Fry Daddy" or other fryer in hot oil until light brown. Cool wontons, wrap in plastic wrap, place in freezer bags, and freeze using freezer bag method.

Serving Day

Place frozen wontons on a baking sheet and bake at 400 degrees for 8–10 minutes or until heated through. Serve with sweet and sour sauce or hot mustard for dipping.

Hot Soft Pretzels

A fun treat for any party

	x3	x6	x9
2 t. active dry yeast	2T	¼c	¼c + 2T
1 T. dark brown sugar, divided	3T	¼c + 2T	½c + 1T
1½ cups very warm water (110 degrees F.)	4½c	9c	13½c
1 T. salt	3T	¼c + 2T	½c + 1T
4 cups all-purpose flour	12c	24c	36c
¼ cup coarse kosher salt	¾c	1½c	2¼c
cornmeal and extra flour for dusting			

Original Recipe Yield

24 pretzels

Cooking Day

In a large bowl, combine yeast, 1½ t. brown sugar, and water and let stand for 5 minutes, until foamy and bubbly. Add remaining sugar and salt and stir well. Add the flour 1 cup at a time, mixing by hand until well incorporated. Knead dough until smooth and elastic, about 7 minutes. Transfer dough to a greased bowl and let stand in a warm place, covered, for 40 minutes. Wrap dough in plastic wrap, place in freezer bag, and freeze, using freezer bag method.

Serving Day

Defrost dough slightly either in microwave on defrost setting or by thawing on countertop. Dust your work surface with flour and cornmeal. Divide dough into approximately 12 pieces and roll each piece out into ropes of desired length and thickness. (Note: thinner = crispier.) Form dough ropes into pretzel shapes and transfer to a baking sheet that has been lightly dusted with cornmeal. Allow pretzels to rise for 30 minutes, uncovered.

Preheat oven to 425 degrees. Bring a large pot of water to a boil. Carefully transfer risen pretzels to boiling water with a spatula and boil on one side for 2 minutes; flip and boil other side for 1½ minutes. Transfer boiled pretzels to a cooling rack to drain for 1 minute. Arrange pretzels on a baking sheet lightly dusted with cornmeal, and sprinkle pretzels with kosher salt. Bake for 20 minutes or until golden brown.

Incredible Crab Cakes

Serve with fresh chili lime aioli—they disappear fast! Can also be made with "fake" crab.

Contributed by Pam Zundel—Lakewood, Colorado

	x2	x4	x6
Crab cakes			
2 T. olive oil	¼c	½c	¾c
⅓ cup diced celery	⅔c	1⅓c	2c
½ medium onion, chopped	1	2	3
1 lb. crab meat (King Phillips or similar brand) or "fake" crab, chopped and shredded	2 lbs	4 lbs	6 lbs
½ cup mayonnaise (more if needed)	1c+	2c+	3c+
2 T. fresh Italian parsley or cilantro	¼c	½c	¾c
1 T. chives	2T	¼c	¼c + 2T
¼ t. salt	½t	1t	1½t
¼ t. pepper	½t	1t	1½t
2 t. Old Bay seasoning	4t	2T + 2t	¼c
1 t. Worcestershire sauce	2t	1T + 1t	2T
1 T. Dijon mustard	2T	¼c	¼c + 2T
1 cup panko breadcrumbs (Japanese breadcrumbs)*	2c	4c	6c
Breading			
6 T. flour	¾c	1½c	2¼c
4 eggs, beaten	8	16	24
4 cups panko breadcrumbs*	8c	16c	24c
canola oil (for frying)			
Serving Day: Chili Lime Aioli			
1 clove garlic, minced			
1 t. kosher salt			

1 large egg
1 large egg yolk
1 cup canola oil
zest of one lime
2 T. fresh lime juice
2 orange or red habanera chili peppers, minced, seeds and ribs removed

*The real key to the taste and success of the crab cakes is the panko breadcrumbs. Regular breadcrumbs may be used, but will not give you the crispy, crunchy texture when baked. Panko breadcrumbs are found in the Asian/Ethnic section of most major supermarkets.

Original Recipe Yield

Makes 30 appetizer-size (1½–2 inch rounds) or 6–8 entrée-size (3–4 inch rounds).

Cooking Day

Crab cakes: Heat olive oil in skillet. Add celery and onions and sauté until soft. In a large bowl, mix the celery and onion with the remainder of ingredients. If needed, add more mayonnaise so the mixture will stick together. Shape into rounds. Set aside.

Breading: In three separate bowls or plates, place the following ingredients in order. 1st bowl: flour; 2nd bowl: beaten eggs; 3rd bowl: panko breadcrumbs.

Dip each crab cake round in flour, then egg, then panko breadcrumbs. Chill for 1–2 hours. Fry crab cakes in approx. ½ inch of canola oil for about 2–3 minutes on each side (approx. 350 degrees if using an electric fry pan, or medium to medium-high heat for stovetop). Drain on paper towel.

Stack crab cakes between layers of parchment paper or wax paper. Place in freezer bag and seal tightly; date and label. Freeze, using freezer bag method.

Serving Day

Crab cakes can be heated directly from the freezer. If frozen, bake at 375 degrees for 15–20 minutes or until heated through; drain on paper towel. If thawed, bake for 10–15 minutes or until heated through. Serve with Chili Lime Aioli (this is best made the day you are serving the crab cakes).

Chili Lime Aioli: Place garlic and salt in food processor or blender and purée. Add egg and egg yolk—process again. With machine running, slowly add canola oil a few drops at a time at first, and then in a thin steady stream. It will emulsify and thicken. Once the oil is added and the aioli has formed, quickly add lime zest and juice and pulse to mix (don't over-mix). Transfer to bowl and stir in the peppers. This may be refrigerated in an airtight container for up to one week. Makes 1½ cups.

Serving Suggestions

For a luncheon or part of a dinner course: The crab cakes are very impressive served over a bed of mixed greens with a small dollop of aioli. To assemble: Drizzle a small amount of light raspberry vinaigrette over the greens. Place one or two crab cakes on top of greens, with a small dollop of aioli on each. (Kraft makes a good light raspberry vinaigrette.)

Mushroom Cap Delights

These get rave reviews at any gathering!

	x3	x6	x9
8 oz. cream cheese, softened	24oz	48oz	72oz
2 egg yolks	6	12	18
1 clove garlic, minced	3	6	9
⅛ t. salt	⅜t	¾t	1⅛t

Serving Day
15 slices of white bread
1 lb. mushroom caps
¼ cup butter
paprika (for garnish)

Original Recipe Yield

60 appetizers

Cooking Day

In food processor or medium mixing bowl, combine cream cheese and egg yolks. Add garlic and salt, and blend well. Freeze, using freezer bag method.

Serving Day

Thaw cream cheese mixture. Cut four 1 inch rounds from each slice of bread. Place on cookie sheet and toast each round lightly on one side under the broiler. Thinly coat the untoasted side of bread rounds with cream cheese mixture.

Sauté mushroom caps in butter; drain on paper towels. Place one mushroom cap on top of each prepared bread round (toasted side down) and fill cap with remaining cheese mixture. Sprinkle with paprika for color, if desired. Broil lightly until browned.

Santa Fe Chicken Nachos

A great upgrade from chips and salsa!

	x3	x6	x9
3 lbs. boneless chicken breast, uncooked, cut into bite-size pieces	9 lbs	18 lbs	27 lbs
24 oz. salsa, mild or medium, to taste	72oz	144oz	216oz
1–15 oz. can black beans, rinsed and drained	3	6	9

Serving Day
8 oz. cream cheese
tortilla chips
grated cheddar cheese
shredded lettuce
diced tomatoes

Original Recipe Yield

6–8 servings

Cooking Day

Combine chicken, salsa, and black beans. Freeze, using freezer bag method.

Serving Day

Thaw completely. Place in slow cooker and cook on low 6–8 hours, until chicken is tender. Prior to serving, add cream cheese and melt completely. Line a 10 x 15 jellyroll pan or a cookie sheet with tortilla chips. Spoon chicken mixture over tortilla chips, then top with grated cheese. Heat in 350 degree oven until cheese is melted. Top with lettuce and tomatoes. Chicken may also be served as an entrée over rice with grated cheese.

Spinach and Cheese in Puff Pastry

Elegant, yet easy!

	x3	x6	x9
2 frozen puff pastry sheets	6	12	18
6 oz. cream cheese, softened	18oz	36oz	54oz
2 t. onion salt	2T	¼c	¼c + 2T
2 cups fresh spinach leaves, torn	6c	12c	18c
4 oz. sun-dried tomatoes, drained	12oz	24oz	36oz
½ cup parmesan cheese	1½c	3c	4½c
½ cup mozzarella cheese	1½c	3c	4½c

Serving Day

1 egg, beaten

Original Recipe Yield

20 servings

Cooking Day

Allow frozen pastry sheets to thaw in refrigerator. When dough is at a workable temperature, roll out each pastry sheet to 12 x 12 inches. Cut pastry sheet in three equal-sized strips (approx. 4 inches wide each). Spread cream cheese down the center of each pastry strip. Sprinkle onion salt over cream cheese. Lightly press spinach leaves into cream cheese. Next sprinkle on sun-dried tomatoes, followed by the parmesan and mozzarella cheeses. Bring both long sides of puff pastry over mixture and press edges together to seal. Seal ends of pastry rolls. Wrap pastry rolls in plastic wrap and place in freezer bags. Freeze, using freezer bag method.

Serving Day

Preheat oven to 425 degrees. Thaw pastry slightly by allowing it to sit at room temperature for 20–30 minutes. Brush beaten egg over pastry rolls. Place rolls on greased baking sheet. Bake in oven for 10–12 minutes or until pastry has risen and is golden brown. If dough begins to brown too much before the pastry has risen, cover lightly with foil during final minutes of baking. Remove from oven and cut into 10 slices per pastry.

Tex Mex Chili Dip

Keep this quick dip on hand;
it's always a hit—great during football games!

	x3	x6	x9
1–15 oz. can chili with no beans	3	6	9
8 oz. cream cheese, cubed	24oz	48oz	72oz
1–7 oz. can diced green chiles, drained*	3	6	9
3 cups Mexican blend cheese (Monterey jack and cheddar)	9c	18c	27c
1 T. chopped green onions	3T	¼c + 2T	½c + 1T
Serving Day			
Tortilla chips for dipping			

*½ cup fresh roasted chiles may be diced and substituted for the canned green chiles.

Original Recipe Yield

6–8 servings

Cooking Day

In a medium, microwave-safe mixing bowl, mix together chili and cream cheese. Microwave on high for 1–2 minutes and stir quickly, just enough to soften the cream cheese and incorporate the chili. Don't worry that it's not hot or completely melted. Spread this mixture into the bottom of a lined 9 x 9 or 7 x 11 baking dish. Next, layer the diced green chiles, then top with cheese. Sprinkle green onions on top of cheese layer. Freeze, using the foil and plastic wrap method.

Serving Day

Unwrap dip, return to baking dish, and thaw slightly. To bake dip in oven, preheat oven to 350 degrees. Bake for 35–45 minutes or until hot, bubbly, and heated completely through. For microwave: Cook on medium-high for 4–5 minutes, rotating once or twice, until mixture is room temperature. Then cook on high for 4–7 minutes, rotating once or twice, until mixture is hot, bubbly, and heated completely through. Serve with tortilla chips or strips. This dip can be reheated again as needed. Any leftover dip stores well in the fridge for 2–3 days. The dip is also excellent used as "filler" inside flour tortillas.

Way Out West Wontons

A delicious southwestern taste

	x2	x4	x6
1 lb. ground beef	2 lbs	4 lbs	6 lbs
½ cup onion, chopped	1c	2c	3c
1–7 oz. can green chiles, drained	2	4	6
2 t. green pepper or jalapeno pepper, chopped (optional)	1T + 1t	2T + 2t	¼c
⅓ cup refried beans (optional)	⅔c	1⅓c	2c
¼ cup cheddar cheese, shredded	½c	1c	1½c
1 T. ketchup	2T	¼c	¼c + 2T
1½ t. chili powder	1T	2T	3T
¼ t. ground cumin	½t	1t	1½t
⅛ t. cayenne pepper (more if you like it hotter)	¼t	½t	¾t
1 t. brown sugar	2t	1T + 1t	2T
1 package wonton skins (small or large)	2	4	6
cooking oil for frying			

Serving Day

salsa, guacamole, and sour cream for dipping

Original Recipe Yield

36 small wontons or 14–18 large wontons

Cooking Day

For filling: In a large skillet, cook ground beef, onion, chiles, and green or jalapeno pepper until meat is brown and vegetables are tender. Drain off any fat. Stir beans (if using), cheese, ketchup, chili powder, cumin, cayenne pepper, and brown sugar into the meat and mix well.

Place a wonton skin on a flat surface with the point toward you. For small wonton skins, place about 2 t. of the meat mixture onto the center of the wonton skin. Fold bottom point of skin over the filling. Seal the sides using your fingertip moistened in a small cup of warm water. Repeat with remaining wonton skins and filling. For larger wonton skins, place 1–2 T. meat mixture on skin and seal using same procedure as above, or you can roll them up like a small package. Place wontons in a single layer in a freezer bag and freeze using freezer bag method.

Serving Day

Remove desired quantity of wontons from freezer. Heat 2–3 inches of cooking oil in an electric skillet or frying pan. When oil is hot, fry the wontons a few at a time, about 1 minute per side or until golden brown. Use a slotted spoon to remove wontons and drain on paper towels. Serve warm with salsa, guacamole, and sour cream.

Bountiful Breads and Brunch

Apricot-Pistachio Oat Bars
Bacon and Egg Strata
Baked Breakfast Blintz
Blueberry Sour Cream Pound Cake
Breakfast Sausage and Apples
Breakfast Strudel
Cheesy Breadsticks
Chicken and Broccoli Quiche
Cinnamon Bread Soufflé with Maple Butter Syrup
Double Dutch Cupcakes
Frozen Fruit Cups
Garlic Herb Bread
Heavenly Scones
Lake Powell Chile Relleno Bake
Old Fashioned Biscuits
Poppy Seed Bread with Orange Glaze
Savory Sausage Bread
Smothered Baked Breakfast Burritos
Sour Cream Coffee Cake
Steve's Chorizo and Egg Burritos

Apricot-Pistachio Oat Bars

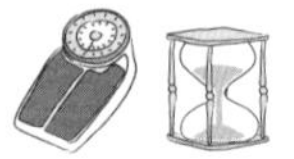

A healthy snack for the freezer!

	x3	x6	x9
nonstick cooking spray			
½ cup all-purpose flour	1½c	3c	4½c
½ cup regular or quick cooking rolled oats	1½c	3c	4½c
⅓ cup packed brown sugar	1c	2c	3c
¼ cup butter, melted	¾c	1½c	2¼c
¾ cup sweetened condensed milk	2¼c	4½c	6¾c
½ t. cinnamon	1½t	1T	4½t
1 cup flaked coconut	3c	6c	9c
1 cup shelled, dry-roasted pistachio nuts	3c	6c	9c
1 cup raisins	3c	6c	9c
1 cup dried apricots, snipped	3c	6c	9c

Original Recipe Yield

16 bars

Cooking Day

Preheat oven to 325 degrees. Line an 8 x 8 x 2 baking pan with foil, extending foil over pan edges. Lightly coat foil with nonstick cooking spray; set aside. In a medium bowl, combine flour, oats, and brown sugar. Stir in butter until mixture clings together. Press ¾ cup of the oat mixture into bottom of pan.

For filling: In a small saucepan over low heat bring condensed milk and cinnamon to boiling. In a bowl, combine coconut, pistachios, raisins, and apricots; add the condensed milk mixture. Stir to combine. Pour coconut mixture into pan over oat layer, using a spatula to spread evenly. Sprinkle remaining oat mixture over filling.

Bake for 30 minutes or until lightly golden. Cool on a rack for 5 minutes. Lift from pan by foil edges; cool completely. Cut into rectangles. Wrap bars in plastic wrap in groups of 2 or 3. Freeze, using freezer bag method.

Serving Day

Allow to thaw and serve with tea or milk for a delicious snack!

Lighter Fare Nutritional Information (per bar): Calories 247; Total Fat 10g; Sodium 63mg; Total Carbohydrates 37g; Dietary Fiber 3g

Bacon and Egg Strata

Bonnie makes this every Easter for Sunday brunch

	x3	x6	x9
1 lb. bacon, fried, drained, and cut into bite-size pieces	3 lbs	6 lbs	9 lbs
9 eggs, slightly beaten	27	54	81
3 cups milk	9c	18c	27c
1 t. salt	1T	2T	3T
½ t. dry mustard	1½t	1T	4½t
3 slices fresh bread, cubed	9	18	27
1½ cups cheddar cheese, grated	4½c	9c	13½c

Original Recipe Yield

8–10 servings

Cooking Day

Mix all ingredients together and place in freezer bag. Freeze, using freezer bag method.

Serving Day

Thaw completely. Place mixture in a greased 9 x 13 baking dish. Bake uncovered at 350 degrees for 1 hour or until golden brown.

Baked Breakfast Blintz

A delicious addition to a breakfast or brunch buffet—top with your favorite preserves or pie filling, and serve with side of bacon or sausage

	x3	x6	x9
Filling			
8 oz. pkg. cream cheese, softened	24oz	48oz	72oz
1 cup low-fat, small-curd cottage cheese	3c	6c	9c
1 egg, beaten	3	6	9
1 T. sugar	3T	¼c + 2T	½c + 1T
1 t. vanilla extract	1T	2T	3T
Batter			
½ cup butter or margarine (room temperature)	1½c	3c	4½c
⅓ cup sugar	1c	2c	3c
4 eggs	12	24	36
1 cup flour	3c	6c	9c
2 t. baking powder	2T	¼c	¼c + 2T
1 cup plain yogurt	3c	6c	9c
½ cup low-fat sour cream	1½c	3c	4½c
½ cup orange juice	1½c	3c	4½c

Suggested toppings for serving day

fresh or canned berry preserves, fresh raspberries, cherry or blueberry pie filling, sour cream or yogurt, and powdered sugar

Original Recipe Yield

8 servings

Cooking Day

Butter and flour a 9 x 13 baking dish or a disposable foil baking pan. Preheat oven to 375 degrees.

Filling: In a small bowl, combine softened cream cheese, cottage cheese, egg, sugar, and vanilla extract. Mix well and set aside.

Batter: In a large bowl, cream together butter and sugar. Add eggs one at a time, beating well after each addition. Stir in the flour and baking powder until just blended. Mix in yogurt, sour cream, and orange juice. Pour half of the batter into the bottom of the prepared baking dish. Spoon the filling mixture over the batter, and then carefully pour the remaining batter over filling. Bake for 45–50 minutes or until lightly browned. Cool completely, cover baking dish with a layer of plastic wrap, then with foil, and freeze.

Serving Day

Remove from freezer and allow to thaw overnight in the refrigerator. To reheat, bake in a preheated 325 degree oven for 20–25 minutes or until heated through. If the top begins to brown too quickly, tent with foil. To serve, cut into squares and serve with the suggested toppings and powdered sugar.

Blueberry Sour Cream Pound Cake

A Martinez family favorite when served warm as side bread or dessert

	x3	x6	x9
nonstick cooking spray			
3 T. dry breadcrumbs	½c + 1T	1c + 2T	1½c + 3T
4 cups flour	12c	24c	36c
¼ t. salt	¾t	1½t	2¼t
1½ cups light sour cream	4½c	9c	13½c
1 t. baking soda	1T	2T	3T
¾ cup butter, softened	2¼c	4½c	6¾c
2¾ cups sugar	8¼c	16½c	24¾c
2 t. vanilla	2T	¼c	¼c + 2T
3 eggs	9	18	27
2 T. fresh lemon juice*	¼c	½c	¾c
1 cup blueberries, fresh or frozen	3c	6c	9c

*This measurement, when multiplied, has been adjusted to accommodate the intensified flavor of acidic ingredients when recipes are made in quantity.

Original Recipe Yield

One 10 inch tube cake or two medium loaf pans.

Cooking Day

Preheat oven to 350 degrees. Coat a 10 inch tube pan or two medium loaf pans with cooking spray and dust with breadcrumbs. In a medium bowl, stir together flour and salt and set aside. In a separate mixing bowl, combine sour cream and baking soda; stir well. Place butter in a large mixing bowl and beat until light and fluffy. Gradually add sugar and vanilla, beating until well blended. Add eggs, 1 at a time, beating well after each addition. Add lemon juice and beat 30 seconds. Add flour mixture alternately with sour cream mixture, beating at low speed. Begin and end this process with flour mixture.

Fold blueberries into batter. Spoon batter into prepared pan. Bake at 350 degrees for 70 minutes or until wooden toothpick inserted in center comes out clean. Cool in pan for 10 minutes on a wire rack; remove from pan. Cool completely and freeze, using instructions for baked goods.

Serving Day

Allow cake to thaw, and serve.

Breakfast Sausage and Apples

A delicious combination to go along with breakfast or brunch!

	x3	x6	x9
1 lb. link sausage (turkey, beef, or pork)	3 lbs	6 lbs	9 lbs
6 medium baking apples, peeled and sliced	18	36	54
1 T. fresh lemon juice*	2T	¼c	¼c + 2T
3 T. brown sugar	½c + 1T	1c + 2T	1½c + 3T
¼ t. salt	¾t	1½t	2¼t
¼ t. pepper (or to taste)	¾t	1½t	2¼t

*This measurement, when multiplied, has been adjusted to accommodate the intensified flavor of acidic ingredients when recipes are made in quantity.

Original Recipe Yield

5–6 servings

Cooking Day

Brown the sausages and cut each link in half crosswise. Drain off excess grease. In a large bowl, combine apples, lemon juice, brown sugar, salt, and pepper, mixing to coat the apples. Gently fold in the sausages. Freeze, using freezer bag method.

Serving Day

Thaw mixture slightly. Grease a 1½ quart baking dish. Preheat oven to 350 degrees. Place apple and sausage mixture into the dish. Cover with foil and bake for 20–25 minutes. Remove foil and stir mixture. Continue baking uncovered for 25–30 more minutes, until apples are soft and caramelized. Stir as needed. Serve with your favorite egg dish.

Breakfast Strudel

A beautiful and delicious breakfast presentation!

Contributed by Mary Sares—Englewood, Colorado

	x2	x4
4 frozen puff pastry sheets*	8	16
11 eggs	22	44
2 T. fresh chives or green onions, chopped	¼c	½c
2 T. unsalted butter	¼c	½c
1 cup frozen hash brown potatoes	2c	4c
1 cup red and/or green bell peppers, diced	2c	4c
1 cup sausage, browned (turkey, pork, or beef)	2c	4c
1 t. salt (or to taste)	2t	1T + 1t
1 t. pepper (or to taste)	2t	1T + 1t
4 oz. cream cheese, softened	8oz	16oz
1 egg, beaten	2	4
1 T. water	2T	¼c

*These are found in the frozen food section of most grocery stores.

Original Recipe Yield

4 strudels

Cooking Day

Thaw pastry sheets to room temperature, about 30 minutes. In a large mixing bowl, whisk eggs and chives (or green onions) together. Set aside. In a large skillet, melt butter over medium-high heat. Add potatoes and peppers; sauté 5 minutes. Add sausage and blend. Add egg mixture to the skillet and scramble just until set. Season with salt and pepper. Take egg mixture off burner and stir in cream cheese. Cool.

Unfold each pastry sheet onto a piece of waxed or parchment paper that has been lightly dusted with flour. Trim the pastry as shown in figure 1. Fill each pastry by spreading egg filling down the center, dividing egg mixture evenly between each pastry sheet. Braid each pastry as shown in figure 2.

Mix remaining egg and water together. Brush each strudel with egg mixture. Wrap each strudel in a layer of plastic wrap, then a layer of foil, and freeze.

Serving Day

Thaw strudel. Preheat oven to 400 degrees. Place strudel on a greased baking sheet and bake for 20–30 minutes or until golden. Cool 5 minutes before slicing.

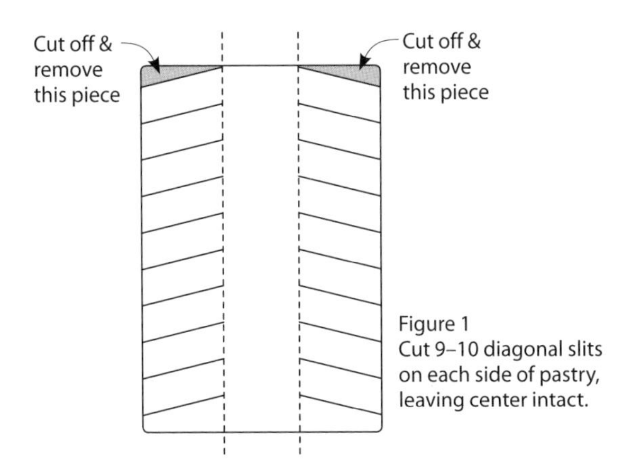

Figure 1
Cut 9–10 diagonal slits on each side of pastry, leaving center intact.

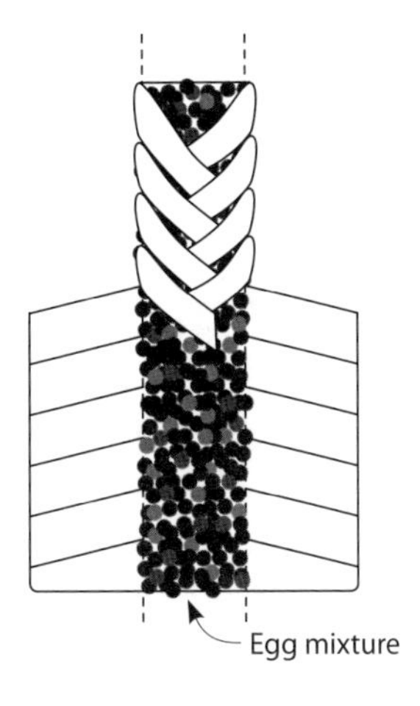

Figure 2
Braid by folding over one strip from right side, then left side. Continue until all strips are braided. Tuck in/under bottom, press to seal.

Cheesy Breadsticks

A wonderful complement to a hot bowl of soup

	x3	x6	x9
1–1 lb. loaf frozen white bread dough, thawed	3	6	9
½ cup freshly grated parmesan cheese	1½c	3c	4½c
¼ cup finely shredded cheddar cheese	¾c	1½c	2¼c
½ t. Italian seasoning	1½t	1T	4½t
½ t. garlic powder	1½t	1T	4½t
¼ t. onion powder	¾t	1½t	2¼t
¼ cup olive oil	¾c	1½c	2¼c

Original Recipe Yield

16 breadsticks

Cooking Day

Divide bread dough into 16 pieces. Roll each piece into a 6 inch rope. Mix together cheeses, Italian seasoning, garlic powder, and onion powder. Coat each bread dough rope in olive oil, then roll in cheese mixture. Grease baking sheets well with additional olive oil. Place ropes 2 inches apart on baking sheets. Let dough rest on baking sheets for 10 minutes. Bake in a 400 degree oven for 10–12 minutes or until golden brown, being careful not to over-bake. Freeze, using instructions for baked goods.

Serving Day

Remove breadsticks from freezer and thaw. Wrap breadsticks in foil or place on baking sheets. Reheat breadsticks in a 300 degree oven until warm.

Chicken and Broccoli Quiche

A hearty quiche for brunch or dinner

	x3	x6	x9
2 cups chicken, cooked and shredded	6c	12c	18c
¾ lb. fresh broccoli, chopped	2¼ lbs	4½ lbs	6¾ lbs
or 1–10 oz. pkg frozen broccoli, thawed, chopped, and drained	3	6	9
1½ cups grated mozzarella (or gruyere)	4½c	9c	13½c
½ cup onion, diced	1½c	3c	4½c
3 eggs	9	18	27
¾ cup cream (or half-and-half)	2¼c	4½c	6¾c
1½ T. fresh lemon juice*	¼c	½c	¾c
1 t. salt	1T	2T	3T
½ t. pepper	1½t	1T	1T + 1½t
1–9 inch pastry shell, unbaked	3	6	9
oil, for sautéing			

*This measurement, when multiplied, has been adjusted to accommodate the intensified flavor of acidic ingredients when recipes are made in quantity.

Original Recipe Yield

5–6 main dish servings

Cooking Day

In a small pan, sauté onions in 1–2 t. oil until almost tender. If you are using fresh broccoli, remove woody stems and microwave 3–5 minutes, or cook broccoli in 1 inch of water 10–12 minutes or until crisp tender. Drain well and chop. Arrange broccoli and onions in bottom of pastry shell, then layer with chicken and cheese.

In a separate bowl, beat eggs, cream, lemon juice, salt, and pepper until combined. Pour into pastry shell. Bake at 375 degrees for 35–45 minutes or until center of quiche is just set. If crust begins to brown, use foil strips around pie edges to prevent over-browning. Cool completely. Cover pie plate with plastic wrap and then foil. Freeze. *If you are serving this on the same day, let quiche stand for 30 minutes before slicing, otherwise it may be too watery. Quiche keeps well in the refrigerator for 2–3 days.*

Serving Day

Thaw quiche. Place in 325 degree oven for 20–30 minutes or until heated through. Cover loosely with a sheet of foil if crusts begin to over-brown. Remove foil for last 3–5 minutes of cooking. Serve with fruit or a salad.

Cinnamon Bread Soufflé with Maple Butter Syrup

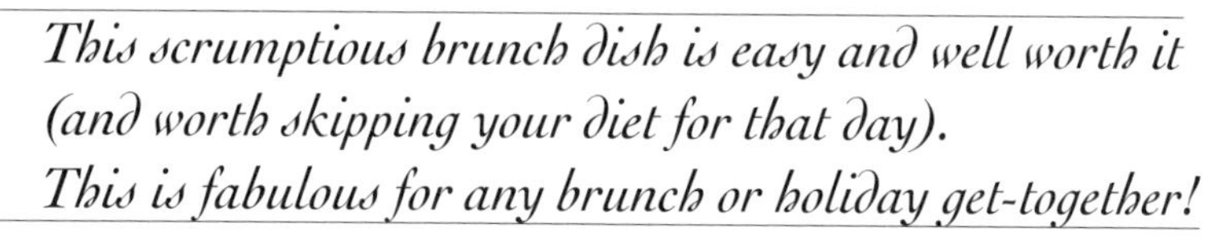
This scrumptious brunch dish is easy and well worth it (and worth skipping your diet for that day). This is fabulous for any brunch or holiday get-together!

	x3	x6	x9
1 loaf cinnamon bread, cut into 1 inch cubes (with or without raisins)	3	6	9
5 eggs	15	30	45
1 cup whole milk or cream	3c	6c	9c
½ cup maple syrup, divided	1½c	3c	4½c
6 oz. cream cheese, softened	18oz	36oz	54oz
3 T. butter, softened	½c + 1T	1c + 2T	1½c + 3T
cinnamon for dusting			

Serving Day
1 cup maple syrup
½ cup butter
powdered sugar for dusting

Original Recipe Yield

6 servings

Cooking Day

Layer cinnamon bread cubes, up to 2 layers thick, in the bottom of a greased 8 x 8 baking dish or a disposable foil baking pan.

In a medium bowl, beat the eggs, milk or cream, and ⅓ c. of the maple syrup until well blended. Pour this mixture over bread cubes. In a small mixing bowl, beat softened cream cheese, butter and remaining maple syrup together until fluffy. Spread this over the bread/egg mixture. Dust with cinnamon. Cover baking dish with a layer of plastic wrap, then foil, and freeze. *If serving fresh, refrigerate overnight.*

Serving Day

Thaw soufflé slightly. Preheat oven to 350 degrees. Bake for 55–60 minutes, or until center of soufflé is set.

While soufflé is baking, prepare maple butter syrup by heating 1 cup maple syrup and ½ cup butter until butter is melted. Dust finished soufflé with powdered sugar and cut into squares. Serve hot, accompanied by the hot buttered syrup.

Double Dutch Cupcakes

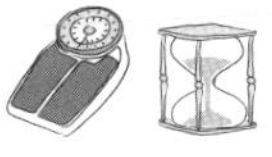

Don't let the name or taste fool you—these delicious cupcakes are actually a light version, studded with bits of dark chocolate. They don't even need frosting!

	x2
2 cups all-purpose flour	4c
⅔ cup unsweetened cocoa (use a high quality cocoa)	1⅓c
2 t. baking soda	1T + 1t
¼ t. salt	½t
1⅓ cups granulated sugar	2⅔c
½ cup butter, softened	1c
1 cup egg substitute	2c
2 t. vanilla	1T + 1t
1 cup low-fat buttermilk	2c
2½ oz. dark (70 percent cocoa) chocolate bar, finely chopped	5oz

Serving Day

¼ cup powdered sugar

Original Recipe Yield

24 cupcakes

Cooking Day

To keep cupcakes light and airy, make this recipe in small batches.

Preheat oven to 350 degrees. In a medium bowl, combine flour, unsweetened cocoa, baking soda, and salt together with a whisk; set aside. Place sugar and butter in a large bowl and beat with a mixer on medium speed until well combined, approximately 2–3 minutes. Add egg substitute and vanilla to the butter/sugar mixture and beat well. To this mixture, alternately add the flour mixture and buttermilk, starting and ending with the flour. With a spatula, gently fold in the dark chocolate bits. Spoon batter into lined muffin cups. Bake for 15–18 minutes or until a wooden toothpick inserted in the center comes out clean. Do not over-bake. Remove cupcakes from pans and cool completely on a wire rack. To freeze, wrap cupcakes in plastic wrap either individually or in sets of 6 and place inside a freezer bag.

Serving Day

Bring cupcakes to room temperature before serving, keeping them wrapped or in a covered container to avoid drying out. Dust with powdered sugar just before serving.

Lighter Fare Nutritional Information (per serving): Calories 150; Total Fat 5.2g; Cholesterol 11mg; Sodium 125mg; Total Carbohydrates 24g; Dietary Fiber 1.1g

Frozen Fruit Cups

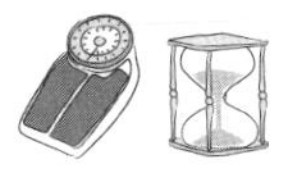

These are beautiful for a light brunch or dessert

Contributed by Suzanne Berg—Littleton, Colorado

	x3	x6	x9
20 oz. frozen strawberries, sliced and thawed	60oz	120oz	180oz
12 oz. frozen orange juice concentrate, slightly thawed	36oz	72oz	108oz
2–20 oz. cans crushed pineapple	6	12	18
1–16 oz. can mandarin oranges	3	6	9
⅓ cup lemon juice	1c	2c	3c
6 bananas, sliced	18	36	54

Original Recipe Yield

25 fruit cups

Cooking Day

Combine all ingredients, including juices from fruit. Spoon fruit into lined muffin cups and freeze. Once fruit is frozen, place liners with frozen fruit in freezer bags.

Serving Day

Remove from freezer about 30 minutes prior to serving.

Hint

Fresh strawberries or pineapple may be substituted for frozen and canned fruit.

Lighter Fare Nutritional Information (per fruit cup): Calories 17; Total Fat 0g; Cholesterol 0mg; Sodium 1mg; Total Carbohydrates 3g; Dietary Fiber 0g; Protein 0g

Garlic Herb Bread

Excellent served with Mediterranean Lasagna!

	x3	x6	x9
1 medium loaf of bread, French or Italian	3	6	9
1 t. coarse kosher salt (more if needed)	1T	2T	3T
¼ cup butter, melted	¾c	1½c	2¼c
4 small cloves garlic	12	24	36
⅛ t. pepper	⅜t	¾t	1⅛t
Optional toppings			
¼ cup parsley, basil, or oregano, chopped	¾c	1½c	2¼c
½ cup parmesan or Italian blend cheese, shredded	1½c	3c	4½c

Original Recipe Yield

6–8 servings

Cooking Day

To make garlic paste: On a cutting board, coarsely chop garlic and then gather into a pile. Sprinkle about ½ t. salt over the garlic. Place flat side of knife blade on top of garlic (sharp side facing away from you). While pressing down firmly, pull the knife toward you, dragging the edge of the knife against the garlic. Repeat again, adding remaining salt, until a paste is formed. (For food processor or blender: Drop garlic cloves, one at a time, into processor, then add salt. If needed, scrape down sides of bowl and pulse until paste is formed.)

Slice bread loaf in half lengthwise. In a small bowl, combine butter, garlic paste, and pepper. Using a pastry or basting brush, spread the butter mixture on the cut sides of bread halves. *If using optional toppings, spread on one side of loaf.* Place one half of loaf on top of the other, sandwiching the toppings. Freeze, using foil and plastic wrap method.

Serving Day

Unwrap the bread and allow it to come to room temperature. When ready to bake, wrap the bread loaf in foil and place on a baking sheet in a preheated 350 degree oven for 12–15 minutes or until heated through. For crispier bread, do not wrap in foil. Slice and serve.

Heavenly Scones

These are light as a feather and melt in your mouth! Serve with Mock Devonshire Cream and jam. Great for breakfast, brunch, or a luncheon!

Contributed by Bev Wirtz—Elkton, Maryland

	x2
2 cups flour	4c
2 T. sugar	¼c
1 T. baking powder	2T
½ t. salt	1t
6 T. butter	¾c
1 egg, slightly beaten	2
½ cup milk	1c

Serving Day
strawberry or raspberry jam
Mock Devonshire Cream

Original Recipe Yield

12 scones

Cooking Day

For light, fluffy scones, prepare this recipe in smaller batches. Don't work with more than 4 cups of flour per batch. Overworking the flour will result in tough, dry scones.

In a medium bowl, sift together flour, sugar, baking powder, and salt. With a pastry blender (or 2 knives), cut in the butter until mixture is the size of small peas. Make a small well in the middle of the flour mixture and add egg and milk. Mix just until incorporated. Working on a lightly floured surface, shape dough into 2 rounds. Cut each round into 6 pie-shaped wedges. Carefully wrap each wedge in plastic wrap. Place the wedges in a single layer in a large freezer bag and freeze.

Serving Day

Prepare Mock Devonshire Cream. Preheat oven to 425 degrees. Take out desired number of scones, unwrap, and place frozen scones on a lightly greased cookie sheet. (Do not thaw scones.) Bake for 10–12 minutes or until light golden brown. Serve by splitting the scone and topping with a dollop of Mock Devonshire Cream and your favorite jam.

Mock Devonshire Cream

½ cup whipping cream
2 T. powdered sugar
½ cup sour cream

In a chilled bowl, whip cream until medium-stiff peaks form, adding sugar during the last few minutes. Fold in sour cream and blend. Can be made ahead and refrigerated. Mock Devonshire Cream will keep in refrigerator for about 3–4 days. Yield: 1½ cups.

Lake Powell Chile Relleno Bake

Vanda takes this on trips to Lake Powell—it reheats wonderfully! Great served on top of toasted bagels.

	x2	x4	x6
½ lb. breakfast sausage, browned and crumbled (turkey, beef, or pork,)*	1 lb	2 lbs	3 lbs
2 cups cheddar cheese, grated**	4c	8c	12c
2 cups Monterey jack cheese, grated**	4c	8c	12c
8 oz. chopped green chiles, canned and drained or fresh (approx. 1 c.)	16oz	32oz	48oz
4 eggs, divided into egg whites and yolks	8	16	24
⅔ cup milk	1⅓c	2⅔c	4c
1 T. flour	2T	¼c	¼c + 2T
⅛ t. pepper	¼t	½t	¾t
½ t. salt	1t	2t	1T
disposable foil pans for baking			

*This is especially good made with beef sausage links broken into pieces. Beef sausage links are usually found in the frozen meat section of your grocery store, packaged in boxes and fully cooked—just brown and crumble.

**Obviously, this is not a low calorie dish and was created as a breakfast/brunch indulgence. This can be made with lower fat cheese; however, fat-free cheese does not freeze well.

Original Recipe Yield

4–6 servings

Cooking Day

In a large bowl, beat egg whites until stiff peaks form. In a small mixing bowl, combine egg yolks, milk, flour, salt, and pepper. Fold this mixture into the egg whites. Gently add green chiles, cheese, and sausage to the egg mixture, mixing just enough to incorporate all ingredients. Do not over-mix. Pour into a greased 7 x 11 casserole dish or disposable foil pan. Bake at 350 degrees for 30 minutes or until top is light-golden.

Cool completely. Cover surface with plastic wrap, then wrap entire dish in foil. Individual portions of this dish can be frozen by dividing into serving sizes, wrapping in plastic wrap, and placing single portions inside a freezer bag.

Serving Day

Thaw egg dish slightly. Unwrap and bake in a 350 degree oven until heated through, or microwave on a medium power setting, checking every minute or so, until warm. This is great served on toasted bagels—like a breakfast sandwich. Serve with salsa for dipping.

Old Fashioned Biscuits

Pop these into the oven directly from the freezer!

	x3	x6	x9
2 cups flour	6c	12c	18c
1 T. baking powder	3T	¼c + 2T	½c + 1T
2 t. sugar	2T	¼c	¼c + 2T
½ t. cream of tartar	1½t	1T	1T + 1½t
¼ t. salt	¾t	1½t	2¼t
½ cup shortening	1½c	3c	4½c
⅔ cup milk	2c	4c	6c

Original Recipe Yield

10–12 biscuits

Cooking Day

Stir together flour, baking powder, sugar, cream of tartar, and salt. Cut in shortening until mixture resembles coarse crumbs. Make a well in the center of flour mixture; pour in milk. Stir just until dough clings together. Knead gently on a lightly floured surface for 10–12 strokes. Do not over-knead, or biscuits will be tough! Roll out or pat dough into ½ inch thickness. Cut with a 2½ inch biscuit cutter. Stack raw biscuits with plastic wrap between layers and freeze, using freezer bag method.

Serving Day

Preheat oven to 450 degrees. Biscuits may go directly from the freezer to the oven. Place on ungreased baking sheet and bake for 10 minutes or until golden brown. Serve warm.

Hint

These biscuits also make a wonderful base for strawberry shortcake! Serve warm with ice cream, fresh strawberries, and whipped cream on top. Delicious!

Poppy Seed Bread with Orange Glaze

A moist, sweet bread that will melt in your mouth!

	x2	x4	x6
3¼ cups sugar, divided	6½c	13c	19½c
½ cup orange juice	1c	2c	3c
2 t. grated orange peel	1T + 1t	2T + 2t	¼c
3⅓ cups flour	6⅔c	13⅓c	20c
1 T. baking powder	2T	¼c	¼c + 2T
1¼ t. salt	2½t	1T + 2t	2T + 1½t
1⅔ cups vegetable oil	3⅓c	6⅔c	10c
3 large eggs	6	12	18
2 t. almond extract	1T + 1t	2T + 2t	¼c
1⅔ cups milk	3⅓c	6⅔c	10c
2 T. poppy seeds	¼c	½c	¾c

Original Recipe Yield

2 large loaves + 1 small loaf

Cooking Day

Bring 1 cup sugar, orange juice, and orange peel to boil in small, heavy saucepan over medium heat. Stir constantly, until sugar dissolves. Set aside to cool.

Preheat oven to 350 degrees. Whisk flour, baking powder, and salt in a medium bowl. Using an electric mixer, in a large bowl beat remaining sugar, oil, eggs, and almond extract until pale yellow in color. Add flour mixture to sugar mixture alternately with milk. Stir in poppy seeds. Pour into greased baking pans. Bake for 1 hour or until inserted toothpick comes out clean. Remove from oven. Poke holes in bread with toothpick. Gradually spoon orange glaze over hot bread, allowing glaze to soak into bread after each addition. Cool completely in pans. Freeze, using instructions for baked goods.

Serving Day

Thaw using instructions for baked goods and serve.

Savory Sausage Bread

Wonderful with Minestrone Soup!

	x2	x4	x6
1 lb. frozen bread dough, thawed	2 lbs	4 lbs	6 lbs
1 lb. sweet Italian or regular sausage (or turkey sausage)	2 lbs	4 lbs	6 lbs
8 oz. mozzarella cheese, cubed	16oz	32oz	48oz
½ cup grated parmesan cheese	1c	2c	3c
1 egg	2	4	6
1 egg white	2	4	6
¼ t. dried oregano	½t	1t	1½t
¼ t. dried basil	½t	1t	1½t
2 t. dried parsley	1T + 1t	2T + 2t	¼c
¼ t. salt	½t	1t	1½t
¼ t. pepper	½t	1t	1½t
oil for brushing			

Original Recipe Yield

8 servings

Cooking Day

Cook sausage in medium pan and drain. In a large bowl, combine sausage, cheeses, egg, and egg white. Mix well and add parsley, basil, oregano, salt, and pepper. Lightly grease a large baking sheet or round pizza pan. On a lightly floured surface, roll bread dough into the size of a medium pizza. Spread the sausage mixture on top of dough to within 1 inch of edges. Roll up dough like a jellyroll. Place roll on pan and curve into a horseshoe shape. Brush top and sides lightly with oil. Bake in a preheated 350 degree oven for 35–40 minutes or until very light golden brown. Cool completely. Wrap in layer of plastic wrap, then foil. Freeze.

Serving Day

Thaw sausage bread completely, letting it come to room temperature. Reheat on a greased baking sheet in a 325 degree oven for 20–30 minutes or until heated through. To prevent over-browning, make a foil tent over the bread, taking foil off for last 5 minutes of baking. Slice, and serve warm.

Smothered Baked Breakfast Burritos

Great for brunch with a southwestern flair!

	x3	x6	x9
12 eggs	36	72	108
2 T. milk	¼c + 2T	¾c	1c + 2T
½ t. salt	1½t	1T	4½t
¼ t. pepper	¾t	1½t	2¼t
1 T. butter	3T	¼c + 2T	½c + 1T
1 lb. bacon, fried and crumbled	3 lbs	6 lbs	9 lbs
12 fajita-size tortillas	36	72	108
2–15 oz. cans green chili or homemade green chili (see Red Rocks Green Chili, page 109)	6	12	18
4 cups shredded cheddar cheese	12c	24c	36c

Serving Day
lettuce
tomato
sour cream
avocados

Original Recipe Yield

12 servings

Cooking Day

In a medium mixing bowl, blend eggs, milk, salt, and pepper. Whisk until smooth. Melt butter in a medium skillet. Add egg mixture, and scramble eggs. Remove from heat before eggs are dry, and add crumbled bacon. To assemble burritos, warm tortillas on a hot skillet or griddle until flexible, flipping once. Fill each tortilla with ¼ cup of egg mixture, and roll tortillas up burrito style. Place filled tortillas, seam side down, in a lined 9 x 13 baking dish. Spoon green chili over rolled tortillas, then top with shredded cheese. Freeze, using foil and plastic wrap method.

Serving Day

Return unwrapped meal to original baking dish and thaw completely. Bake at 350 degrees for 25–35 minutes, until sauce bubbles and cheese is melted. Top with your choice of lettuce, tomato, sour cream, sliced avocados, or guacamole.

Sour Cream Coffee Cake

Luscious down to the very last crumb!

	x2	x4	x6
Cake			
½ cup butter	1c	2c	3c
1 cup sugar	2c	4c	6c
2 eggs	4	8	12
1 t. vanilla	2t	1T + 1t	2T
1 cup sour cream	2c	4c	6c
2 cups flour	4c	8c	12c
1 t. baking soda	2t	1T + 1t	2T
1 t. baking powder	2t	1T + 1t	2T
½ t. salt	1t	2t	1T
Topping			
3 T. flour	¼c + 2T	¾c	1c + 2T
¾ cup brown sugar	1½c	3c	4½c
1 T. cinnamon	2T	¼c	¼c + 2T
3 T. butter, melted	¼c + 2T	¾c	1c + 2T
¾ cup chopped nuts	1½c	3c	4½c

Original Recipe Yield

12 servings

Cooking Day

For cake batter: Cream together butter and sugar until fluffy. Add eggs, one at a time, beating well after each addition. Add vanilla. Sift together flour, baking powder, baking soda, and salt in a separate bowl; add to the creamed mixture alternately with sour cream, beginning and ending with dry ingredients. Grease an 8 x 8 square baking pan. Place a layer of parchment paper or wax paper in the bottom of pan, then spoon cake batter into baking pan.

For topping: In a separate bowl, mix together topping ingredients. Sprinkle cake batter with topping. Bake at 350 degrees for 30–35 minutes, until toothpick inserted in center comes out clean. Cool in pan for 10 minutes. With a small spatula or butter knife, loosen cake from sides of pan. Invert cake onto plate, then immediately invert onto wire rack to cool completely, crumb side up. Freeze, using instructions for baked goods.

Serving Day

Thaw completely. Cake can be reheated in the microwave on a medium power setting or in a 325 degree oven until warm.

Steve's Chorizo and Egg Burritos

A breakfast favorite of Bonnie's family

	x3	x6	x9
1–12 oz. pkg. beef chorizo	3	6	9
12 eggs, slightly beaten	36	72	108
8 flour tortillas, burrito-size	24	48	72

Original Recipe Yield

8 burritos

Cooking Day

Fry chorizo in large skillet on medium heat until chorizo is cooked and has a saucy consistency. Drain grease according to taste, but do not drain off entire amount, as this will take away from the chorizo flavor. Add beaten eggs to chorizo and scramble, mixing thoroughly. Cook to desired consistency. Warm flour tortillas in a medium hot skillet. Place ¾–1 cup of chorizo and egg mixture on each tortilla, according to desired size of burritos. Roll up tortillas burrito-style. Once burritos are cool, wrap individually in plastic wrap and then place in a freezer bag. Freeze, using freezer bag method.

Serving Day

Remove desired number of burritos from freezer. Heat in microwave on high for 60–90 seconds, or until burritos are warmed through.

Savory Soups

Buffalo Chicken Soup

Bleu cheese and hot pepper sauce make this a wonderfully unique soup

	x3	x6	x9
1–2¼ to 2½ lb. deli-roasted chicken, skinned, boned, and coarsely shredded	3	6	9
or approx. 2½ c. cooked chicken	7½c	15c	22½c
2 T. butter	¼c + 2T	¾c	1c + 2T
½ cup coarsely chopped celery	1½c	3c	4½c
½ cup chopped onion	1½c	3c	4½c
2–14 oz. cans reduced-sodium chicken broth	6	12	18
1½ cups milk	4½c	9c	13½c
1 t. salt	1T	2T	3T
1½ t. bottled hot pepper sauce	4½t	3T	¼c + 1½t
1½ cups shredded mozzarella cheese (6 oz.)	4½c	9c	13½c
1¼ cups crumbled bleu cheese (5 oz.)	3¾c	7½c	11¼c
½ cup shredded parmesan cheese (2 oz.)	1½c	3c	4½c
⅓ cup all-purpose flour	1c	2c	3c

Serving Day

bottled hot pepper sauce (optional)

Original Recipe Yield

6–8 servings

Cooking Day

In a 4-quart Dutch oven, melt butter over medium heat. Add celery and onion; cook and stir until tender. Stir in broth, milk, salt, and hot pepper sauce.

In a medium bowl, toss together mozzarella cheese, bleu cheese, parmesan cheese, and flour. Add gradually to soup, stirring after each addition until just melted. Stir in shredded chicken; heat through but do not allow to boil. Cool completely. Freeze, using freezer bag method.

Serving Day

Thaw soup to a slushy consistency. Reheat in saucepan. Top with additional bleu cheese crumbles and hot sauce if desired.

Chicken, Shrimp, and Sausage Stew

Wonderfully spicy and flavorful; serve with warm bread

	x3	x6	x9
1 lb. andouille sausage, cut into rounds	3 lbs	6 lbs	9 lbs
6 chicken thighs (or 3 boneless chicken breasts), cut into bite-size pieces	18	36	54
2 cups chopped onion	6c	12c	18c
2⅓ cups chopped green bell pepper	7c	14c	21c
1¼ cups chopped red bell pepper	3¾c	7½c	11¼c
6 large garlic cloves, chopped	18	36	54
1 T. dried oregano	3T	¼c + 2T	½c + 1T
2 t. dried thyme	2T	¼c	¼c + 2T
1 T. paprika	3T	¼c + 2T	½c + 1T
2–14 oz. cans diced tomatoes, undrained	6	12	18
1–14 oz. can low-salt chicken broth	3	6	9
1 cup dry white wine	3c	6c	9c
salt and pepper to taste			
⅓ cup sliced stuffed green olives (optional)	1c	2c	3c

Serving Day

1 lb. large, uncooked shrimp, peeled and deveined (optional)

Original Recipe Yield

8 servings

Cooking Day

Sauté sausage in a large, heavy pot or Dutch oven over medium heat until brown, about 4 minutes. Transfer to large bowl. Sprinkle chicken with salt and pepper. Add chicken to pot and cook until browned, about 3 minutes per side. Transfer chicken to bowl with sausage. Pour off all but 1 T. pan drippings.

Add onion and both bell peppers to pot; sauté until onion is golden brown, about 15 minutes. Add garlic, oregano, thyme, and paprika; sauté 2 more minutes. Return sausage and chicken to pot, including any accumulated juices from the bowl. Add tomatoes, chicken broth, and wine. Bring to boil. Reduce heat, cover, and simmer until chicken is cooked through, about 25 minutes.

Uncover pot. Add olives (if using) and simmer until chicken is very tender and liquid is reduced to the consistency of a thin sauce, about 40 minutes. Cool completely. Freeze, using freezer bag method.

Serving Day

Allow soup to thaw to a slushy consistency. Warm soup in a stockpot over medium-low heat until it begins to simmer. If desired, add shrimp and simmer about 5 minutes longer, until shrimp is just cooked. Season to taste with salt and pepper.

Chipotle-Chocolate Chili

A rich and hearty chili that is SO good!

	x3	x6	x9
1 lb. ground beef or turkey	3 lbs	6 lbs	9 lbs
1 cup diced onion	3c	6c	9c
1 cup chopped red bell pepper	3c	6c	9c
1 t. minced garlic	1T	2T	3T
3 T. brown sugar	½c + 1T	1c + 2T	1½c + 3T
2 T. chili powder	¼c + 2T	¾c	1c + 2T
1 T. unsweetened cocoa	3T	¼c + 2T	½c + 1T
1 t. ground cumin	1T	2T	3T
½ t. freshly ground black pepper	1½t	1T	4½t
¼ t. salt	¾t	1½t	2¼t
1–15 oz. can pinto beans, drained	3	6	9
1–15 oz. can kidney beans, drained	3	6	9
2–14.5 oz. cans diced tomatoes, undrained	6	12	18
1–14 oz. can low-sodium chicken broth	3	6	9
½ cup roasted chipotle salsa	1½c	3c	4½c

Serving Day (optional)
1 oz. square semisweet chocolate, chopped
sour cream
green onions

Original Recipe Yield

8 servings

Cooking Day

Add ground beef or turkey, onion, bell pepper, and garlic to stockpot. Cook over medium-high heat until meat is browned and vegetables are tender, approximately 8 minutes. Drain. Add sugar, chili powder, cocoa, cumin, black pepper, salt, pinto beans, kidney beans, tomatoes, broth, and salsa. Stir to blend; bring to a boil over medium-high heat. Reduce heat and simmer for 15 minutes or until slightly thickened. Cool completely. Freeze, using freezer bag method.

Serving Day

Thaw chili and heat thoroughly in saucepan. If more chocolate flavor is desired, add a 1 oz. square of semisweet chocolate, chopped, after chili is removed from heat; stir until melted. Serve with a dollop of sour cream and sliced green onions.

Clam Chowder

Everyone needs a good clam chowder recipe!

	x3	x6	x9
2–6 oz. cans clams	6	12	18
1 cup celery, diced	3c	6c	9c
1 onion, diced	3	6	9
2 cups potatoes, diced	6c	12c	18c
¾ cup butter	2¼c	4½c	6¾c
¾ cup flour	2¼c	4½c	6¾c
1 qt. half-and-half	3qts	1½gals	2gals +1qt
2 t. salt	2T	¼c	¼c + 2T
⅛ t. pepper	⅜t	¾t	1⅛t

Original Recipe Yield

6 servings

Cooking Day

Drain clams, reserving juice. In a stockpot, simmer diced vegetables in reserved clam juice until tender, adding additional water if necessary to cover the vegetables. In a separate stockpot, melt butter and then stir in flour, salt, and pepper until smooth. Add half-and-half to butter and flour, stirring constantly to avoid lumps. Add half-and-half mixture to vegetables and broth. Add clams. Simmer for 10 minutes. Cool completely. Freeze, using freezer bag method.

Serving Day

Thaw completely. Heat on stove until heated through.

Creamy Tomato Basil Soup

A smooth soup that warms the soul

Contributed by Shirley Burke—Westminster, Colorado

	x3	x6	x9
2 medium onions, chopped	6	12	18
4 stalks celery, chopped	12	24	36
4 leaves fresh basil	12	24	36
1 bay leaf	3	6	9
2–28 oz. cans whole tomatoes, undrained	6	12	18
3 T. butter, melted	½c + 1T	1c + 2T	1½c + 3T
¼ cup flour	¾c	1½c	2¼c
2 T. sugar	¼c + 2T	¾c	1c + 2T
2 t. salt	2T	¼c	¼c + 2T
½ t. pepper	1½t	1T	4½t

Serving Day

2 cups nonfat milk
1 t. baking soda

Original Recipe Yield

8 servings

Cooking Day

Combine onions, celery, basil, bay leaf, and tomatoes in stockpot. Simmer until vegetables are tender, about 45–60 minutes. Remove bay leaf. Purée tomato mixture in a blender and then strain through a fine sieve or colander. Return tomato mixture to stockpot. In a small mixing bowl, blend flour and melted butter into a smooth paste, then add a small amount of the tomato mixture. Stir until smooth. Gradually add the flour mixture to stockpot, stirring constantly to avoid scorching and lumps. Add sugar, salt, and pepper. Cool completely. Freeze, using freezer bag method.

Serving Day

Thaw completely. Reheat soup in stockpot, adding milk and baking soda. Heat through, but do not allow to boil.

Lighter Fare Nutritional Information (per 1 cup serving): Calories 156; Total Fat 4.6g; Cholesterol 13mg; Sodium 1182mg; Total Carbohydrates 22g; Dietary Fiber 3g; Protein 5g

Crested Butte Chicken, Chile, and Corn Soup

Delicious and sure to satisfy!

	x3	x6	x9
3½ cups frozen sweet corn (or canned, drained)	10½c	21c	31½c
1 cup chicken stock	3c	6c	9c
¼ cup butter	¾c	1½c	2¼c
2 cups milk	6c	12c	1gal + 2c
1 clove garlic, minced	3	6	9
1 T. fresh oregano (or 1 t. dried)	3T	¼c + 2T	½c + 1T
¼ t. cayenne pepper (optional)	¾t	1½t	2¼t
1–4 oz. can chopped green chiles, drained*	3	6	9
2 cups cooked chicken, chopped or shredded	6c	12c	18c
1 cup tomatoes, diced or puréed	3c	6c	9c
1 cup Monterey or cheddar jack cheese, grated	3c	6c	9c
salt and pepper, to taste			

Serving Day (toppings)

fresh cilantro or parsley, chopped
corn tortilla chips, crushed
sour cream
avocado, diced
shredded cheese

*½ cup fresh-roasted green chiles (mild or medium) may be substituted for canned.

Original Recipe Yield

6–8 servings

Cooking Day

If using frozen corn, cook according to package directions until tender and drain. Combine corn and chicken stock in a blender and purée. In a large stockpot, combine butter with corn mixture and simmer slowly for 5 minutes, stirring occasionally. Add milk, garlic, oregano, cayenne pepper (if using), and salt and pepper to taste; bring to a boil. Reduce heat and add green chiles, simmering for 5 more minutes. Stir in chicken and tomatoes. Remove soup from heat and add cheese, stirring until melted. Cool completely. Freeze, using freezer bag method.

Serving Day

Thaw soup until consistency is slushy. Reheat soup on low heat; do not allow to boil. Serve with your choice of toppings.

Elegant Cream of Mushroom Soup

An unlikely favorite of teens crashing at Susie's house

	x3	x6	x9
1 lb. mushrooms	3 lbs	6 lbs	9 lbs
⅓ cup chopped shallots	1c	2c	3c
2 cloves chopped garlic	6	12	18
2 stalks chopped celery	6	12	18
½ cup unsalted butter, divided	1½c	3c	4½c
½ cup flour	1½c	3c	4½c
6 cups hot chicken broth	18c	36c	54c
½ cup dry cooking sherry	1½c	3c	4½c
¾ cup whipping cream	2¼c	4½c	6¾c
¼ t. cayenne pepper (optional)	¾t	1½t	2¼t
salt and pepper to taste			

Original Recipe Yield

8 servings

Cooking Day

Finely chop half the mushrooms. Slice the remaining half. Sauté shallots, celery, and garlic in half the butter until tender. Add finely chopped mushrooms and sauté until tender, but not brown. Add flour and stir with a wooden spoon until a smooth paste has formed. Reduce heat and cook for 3 minutes, stirring constantly. Gradually add hot chicken broth, stirring constantly with a whisk. Bring to a boil. Simmer 10 minutes. In a separate pan, sauté the sliced mushrooms in remaining butter. Add cooking sherry. Cook until liquid is reduced by approximately half. Add sliced mushrooms to the soup. Simmer 10 more minutes. Add whipping cream and season to taste with salt, pepper, and cayenne pepper. Cool completely and freeze, using freezer bag method.

Serving Day

Thaw soup to slushy consistency. Place in saucepan and heat through, but do not allow soup to boil.

Four Cheese Italian Minestrone

Wonderful served with our Savory Sausage Bread!

	x3	x6	x9
¼ cup olive oil	¾c	1½c	2¼c
1 cup onion, chopped	3c	6c	9c
2 cloves garlic, minced	6	12	18
4 sprigs flat leaf parsley, chopped	12	24	36
2 stalks celery, finely chopped	6	12	18
3 carrots, sliced	9	18	27
8 oz. fresh mushrooms, sliced	24oz	48oz	72oz
5 cups canned tomatoes (diced or puréed)	15c	30c	45c
2 cups beef broth	6c	12c	18c
1 t. oregano	1T	2T	3T
1 t. basil	1T	2T	3T
½ t. salt	1½t	1T	4½t
¼ t. pepper	¾t	1½t	2¼t
1–15 oz. can green beans, undrained	3	6	9
1–15 oz. can cannelloni or great northern beans, undrained	3	6	9
½ lb. sweet Italian turkey sausage, cooked, crumbled, and drained (optional)	1½ lbs	3 lbs	4½ lbs
⅓ cup Italian blend cheese, shredded*	1c	2c	3c

Serving Day

1 cup small tube or elbow pasta

*Italian blend cheese is a blend of parmesan, asiago, Romano, and mozzarella cheeses, and is found among the packaged, refrigerated cheeses in your local grocery store.

Original Recipe Yield:

4–6 servings

Cooking Day

In a stockpot, heat olive oil on medium heat and sauté onions, garlic, parsley, celery, carrots, and mushrooms until crisp tender. Place tomatoes in a blender (if not already puréed) and blend until fairly smooth. Add tomato purée, beef broth, oregano, basil, salt, pepper, green beans, cannelloni/northern beans, and sausage (if using) to the sautéed vegetables. Simmer for 30 minutes. Adjust seasonings according to personal taste. Add Italian cheese and stir until just melted. Cool completely. Freeze, using freezer bag method.

Serving Day

Thaw soup to a slushy consistency. Reheat, simmering, for 20–30 minutes. Meanwhile, cook pasta in water according to package directions. Drain and add to simmering soup. Ladle into bowls and top with additional Italian cheese as desired.

Hearty Corn Chowder

A favorite of Bonnie's family on cold winter nights

	x3	x6	x9
¼ cup butter, melted	¾c	1½c	2¼c
6 T. onions, chopped	1c + 2T	2¼c	3¼c + 2T
¾ cup celery, diced	2¼c	4½c	6¾c
2½ cups hot water	7½c	15c	22½c
2 cups potatoes, peeled and cubed	6c	12c	18c
3 cups frozen kernel corn	9c	18c	27c
2 T. sugar	¼c + 2T	¾c	1c + 2T
2 t. salt	2T	¼c	¼c + 2T
¼ t. pepper	¾t	1½t	2¼t
3 T. flour	½c + 1T	1c + 2T	1½c + 3T
1 quart half-and-half	3qts	1½gals	2gal + 1qt

Serving Day

shredded cheese and bacon pieces for garnish

Original Recipe Yield

9 servings

Cooking Day

Sauté onions and celery in butter until tender. Add water, potatoes, corn, sugar, salt, and pepper. Cover and simmer until potatoes are tender, about 30 minutes. In a small bowl, whisk flour into 1 cup of half-and-half. Stir into soup, then add remaining half-and-half. Heat until desired thickness, stirring frequently. Cool completely and freeze, using freezer bag method.

Serving Day

Thaw completely. Heat on stove until heated through, but do not allow to boil. Top individual bowls with shredded cheese and bacon.

Red Rocks Green Chili

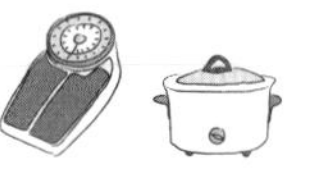

Serve as a soup with warm tortillas—
or as a topping for our Smothered Breakfast Burritos

	x3	x6	x9
2 lbs. pork roast	6 lbs	12 lbs	18 lbs
1 T. vegetable oil	3T	¼c + 2T	½c + 1T
1 medium onion, diced	3	6	9
1 clove garlic, minced	3	6	9
1–14.5 oz can diced tomatoes, undrained	3	6	9
1–15 oz. can tomato sauce	3	6	9
1–10 oz. can Rotel tomatoes, undrained	3	6	9
1–14 oz can diced green chiles, drained	3	6	9
¾ t. salt	2¼t	4½t	2T + ¾t
½ t. black pepper	1½t	1T	4½t
½ t. cumin	1½t	1T	4½t
¼ t. cayenne pepper	¾t	1½t	2¼t

Original Recipe Yield

8 servings

Cooking Day

Cut pork roast into 1 inch cubes. Heat oil in large stockpot or Dutch oven; brown meat, onion, and garlic. Add remaining ingredients and simmer until meat is tender, approximately 2 hours. After meat is browned, chili may also be cooked in the crockpot on a low setting for 4–6 hours. Cool completely and freeze, using freezer bag method.

Serving Day

Thaw completely. Heat on stove until chili is heated through. May be served in bowls and topped with grated cheese. This green chili is also wonderful when served as a topping for smothered burritos or breakfast burritos.

Lighter Fare Nutritional Information (per 1 cup serving): Calories 317; Total Fat 12.8g; Cholesterol 92mg; Sodium 777mg; Total Carbohydrates 13g; Dietary Fiber 2g; Protein 35g

Saucy Vegetable Beef Soup

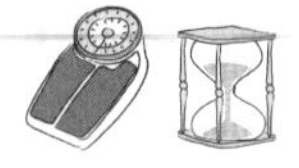

A robust soup that is oh, so good!

	x3	x6	x9
1½ lbs. ground beef	4½ lbs	9 lbs	13½ lbs
1 medium onion, chopped	3	6	9
1 cup celery, diced	3c	6c	9c
2–14 oz. cans beef broth, divided	6	12	18
2 T. steak sauce	¼c + 2T	¾c	1c + 2T
2 t. Worcestershire sauce	2T	¼c	¼c + 2T
1 t. salt	1T	2T	3T
½ t. black pepper	1½t	1T	4½t
¼ cup flour	¾c	1½c	2¼c
1–10 oz. bag frozen mixed vegetables	3	6	9
1–28 oz. can diced tomatoes, undrained	3	6	9

Original Recipe Yield

6–8 servings

Cooking Day

In a large stockpot, brown ground beef with onion and celery until vegetables are tender and meat is browned. Drain. Add 1 can of beef broth, steak sauce, Worcestershire sauce, salt, and pepper. Bring to a boil, then reduce heat and simmer for 20 minutes. In a separate bowl, mix flour with remaining can of beef broth. Once flour and broth are well mixed, add to soup and continue stirring until soup is bubbly. Cook for an additional minute. Stir in mixed vegetables and diced tomatoes. Cool completely and freeze, using freezer bag method.

Serving Day

Thaw completely. Place soup in stockpot. Bring to boil, then simmer until vegetables are tender and soup is heated through, about 20 minutes.

Lighter Fare Nutritional Information (per 1 cup serving): Calories 405; Total Fat 18.5g; Cholesterol 92mg; Sodium 1394mg; Total Carbohydrates 24g; Dietary Fiber 2g; Protein 33g

Sausage with Cheese Tortellini Soup

You can't eat just one bowl!

	x3	x6	x9
2 slices bacon, diced	6	12	18
2 cups onion, chopped	6c	12c	18c
¾ lb. Italian sausage, browned and drained	2¼ lbs	4½ lbs	6¾ lbs
8 cups beef broth	24c	48c	72c
2 T. fresh basil, minced	¼c + 2T	¾c	1c + 2T
½ cup fresh parsley, minced	1½c	3c	4½c
1 clove garlic, pressed	3	6	9
¼ t. cayenne pepper	¾t	1½t	2¼t
¼ t. black pepper	¾t	1½t	2¼t
1–9 oz. package cheese tortellini	3	6	9
2 cups fresh spinach leaves, torn	6c	12c	18c

Serving Day

fresh parmesan cheese and croutons for garnish

Original Recipe Yield

8 servings

Cooking Day

In stockpot, sauté bacon and onion until golden. Add sausage, beef broth, basil, parsley, garlic, cayenne pepper, and black pepper. Bring to boil. Reduce heat and simmer for 10 minutes. In a separate stockpot, cook tortellini according to package directions. Drain. Add tortellini and spinach leaves to soup, then simmer until tortellini is heated through, but do not boil. Remove from heat and cool. Freeze, using freezer bag method.

Serving Day

Thaw completely. Reheat on stove, but do not boil. Garnish soup with fresh parmesan cheese and croutons; serve.

Slow Cooker Split Pea Soup

Delicious with homemade croutons!

Contributed by Tami Hastings—Littleton, Colorado

	x3	x6	x9
1–16 oz. pkg. dried split green peas, rinsed	3	6	9
2 cups diced ham	6c	12c	18c
3 carrots, peeled and sliced	9	18	27
½ cup onion, chopped	1½c	3c	4½c
2 stalks of celery with leaves, chopped	6	12	18
2 cloves garlic, minced	6	12	18
1 bay leaf	3	6	9
¼ cup fresh parsley, chopped	¾c	1½c	2¼c
2 t. seasoned salt	2T	¼c	¼c + 2T
½ t. fresh black pepper	1½t	1T	4½t
1½ qts. hot water	1gal + 2c	2gal + 1qt	3gal + 1½qts
2–14 oz. cans chicken broth	6	12	18

Original Recipe Yield

12 servings

Cooking Day

Layer ingredients in slow cooker in the order given in ingredient list; finish by pouring in water and chicken broth. Do not stir. Cover and cook on low for 5–6 hours or until vegetables are soft. Remove bay leaf. Mash peas to thicken soup, if desired. Cool completely and freeze, using freezer bag method.

Serving Day

Thaw completely. Reheat on stovetop until heated through. Optional: serve garnished with homemade croutons.

Homemade Croutons: Cut 4 slices of bread into ½ inch cubes. Place cubes on a baking sheet. Drizzle with ¼ cup olive oil and 1 t. garlic salt until well coated. Bake in a 350 degree oven for 10–15 minutes, stirring occasionally, until croutons are crisp and golden brown.

Lighter Fare Nutritional Information (per 1 cup serving of soup): Calories 133; Total Fat 5.3g; Cholesterol 14mg; Sodium 1465mg; Total Carbohydrates 10g; Dietary Fiber 0g; Protein 9g

All-Seasons Sesame Chicken

This grilled chicken is made ahead and frozen already cooked. Keep it on hand for salads, sandwiches, or snacks—hot or cold!

	x2	x4	x6
3 lbs. boneless chicken breast (and/or thighs)	6 lbs	12 lbs	18 lbs
½ cup olive oil	1c	2c	3c
½ cup white wine	1c	2c	3c
½ cup soy sauce	1c	2c	3c
2 T. fresh ginger, grated	¼c	½c	¾c
1 T. dry mustard	2T	¼c	¼c + 2T
1 t. fresh ground black pepper	2t	1T + 1t	2T
4 cloves garlic, crushed	8	16	24
½ cup green onion, chopped	1c	2c	3c
3 T. sesame seeds	¼c + 2T	¾c	1c + 2T

Original Recipe Yield

6–8 servings

Cooking Day

Place the chicken in a large freezer bag set inside a bowl (for stability). In another bowl, combine the remaining ingredients and mix well. Pour the marinade over the chicken and seal freezer bag. Refrigerate and marinate for 4–8 hours.

Remove the chicken from the freezer bag, reserving the marinade. In a saucepan, bring marinade to a boil and continue boiling for 2 additional minutes. Grill chicken over medium-hot coals for 15–20 minutes or until chicken is cooked through, turning once. Baste the chicken frequently with marinade. *Do not* over-cook chicken.

Allow the chicken to rest for at least 10 minutes before slicing into strips. Place cooled chicken strips and remaining marinade into portion sized freezer bags. Freeze, using freezer bag method.

Fabulous Poultry and Fish

All-Seasons Sesame Chicken
Baja Grilled Fish Tacos
Balsamic Roasted Chicken Thighs
Bangkok Chicken Satay
Basil Grilled Tuna Kabobs
Bombay Chicken Curry
Cajun Style Chicken Leg Quarters
Calypso Salmon
Chicken Cordon Bleu
Chicken Marsala
Chicken Oreganato
Ginger Glazed Mahi Mahi
Gourmet Salmon Burgers
Grilled Coconut Lime Chicken Tenders
Grilled Honey Lime Chicken
Maui Grilled Chicken Sandwiches
Monterey Jack Stuffed Chicken
Orange Braised Chicken Thighs with Green Olives
Orange Pine Nut Chicken
Parmesan Garlic Chicken
Pineapple Lemon Chicken
Savory Chicken Bundles
Sesame Salmon
South of the Border Chicken Enchiladas
Spicy Peanut Chicken
Teriyaki Chicken Veggie Stir-Fry

Serving Day

Use chicken strips for salads, sandwiches, stir fry, or as a main entrée. Chicken can be eaten cold or hot. To warm, gently reheat in microwave or in oven, covered.

Lighter Fare Nutritional Information (per serving): Calories 409; Total Fat 20g; Cholesterol 112mg; Sodium 1155mg; Total Carbohydrates 5g; Dietary Fiber 1.2g; Protein 47.4g

Baja Grilled Fish Tacos

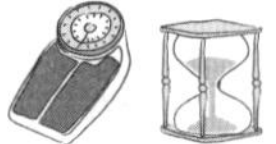

Outstanding flavor—good any time of year!

	x3	x6	x9
1½ lbs. tilapia, striped bass, or similar mild fish fillets	4½ lbs	9 lbs	13½ lbs
1 t. kosher (coarse) salt	1T	2T	3T
½ t. pepper	1½t	1T	4½t
1 large sweet white onion, finely chopped	3	6	9
½ cup fresh cilantro, chopped	1½c	3c	4½c
2 small cloves of garlic, minced	6	12	18
1 t. ground cumin (or more to taste)	1T	2T	3T
1 t. dried oregano	1T	2T	3T
½ cup olive oil	1½c	3c	4½c
¼ cup + 3 T. fresh lime juice*	1¼c	2½c	3¾c
¼ cup fresh orange juice	¾c	1½c	2¼c

Serving Day

- cooking spray or oil
- salsa or pico de gallo
- tortillas, heated
- red onion, chopped
- cilantro, chopped
- avocado, diced
- cabbage, finely shredded
- lime wedges

Baja Lime Cream

- ½ cup mayonnaise
- ½ cup sour cream
- 2 T. fresh lime juice
- 1 t. finely grated lime zest
- 1 T. sugar, or more if needed

salt to taste

pinch of cayenne pepper

*This measurement, when multiplied, has been adjusted to accommodate the intensified flavor of acidic ingredients when recipes are made in quantity.

Original Recipe Yield

6 servings

Cooking Day

Gently rinse fish fillets, then pat dry with paper towels. Sprinkle both sides of fish with kosher salt and pepper. Set aside. In a medium bowl, combine the remaining ingredients. Divide this marinade into three equal portions. Place one third of the marinade in a small freezer bag and set aside. Place the next third of marinade in a larger freezer bag. Place the fish fillets into the larger bag on top of the marinade. Top fillets with the last third of marinade; seal bag. Let the fish marinate in the refrigerator for approximately 20–30 minutes, turning once, before freezing using freezer bag method. Freeze the extra marinade in a separate, smaller bag; keep both bags together in freezer for ease on serving day.

Serving Day

Thaw fish and extra marinade completely. To grill fish: spray grill surface with cooking spray to keep fish from sticking, or place foil that has been lightly sprayed with cooking oil on top of grill. *Fish may also be grilled on a sprayed stovetop griddle pan or broiled in the oven 4 inches from heat, 5 minutes per ½ inch of thickness or until fish flakes.* Grill fish over medium heat, turning only once, and basting fish with extra marinade while grilling. Once the fish is cooked, coarsely chop. Assemble fish tacos using your choice of serving day condiments. Top with a drizzle of Baja Lime Cream.

Baja Lime Cream: Mix together mayonnaise, sour cream, lime juice, lime zest, sugar, salt, and cayenne pepper. Adjust seasonings to taste, adding more sugar if needed. Makes about 1 cup. Refrigerate until ready to serve.

Lighter Fare Nutritional Information (per 1 cup serving of fish): Calories 194; Total Fat 10.9g; Cholesterol 0mg; Sodium 390mg; Total Carbohydrates 5.8g; Dietary Fiber .8g; Protein 21.3g

Balsamic Roasted Chicken Thighs

Prepare in the oven or on the grill

	x3	x6	x9
6 chicken thighs, with bone and skin	18	36	54
½ cup extra virgin olive oil	1½c	3c	4½c
3 T. balsamic vinegar*	½c	1c	1½c
2 garlic cloves, pressed	6	12	18
½ t. salt	1½t	1T	4½t
¼ t. pepper	¾t	1½t	2¼t

*This measurement, when multiplied, has been adjusted to accommodate the intensified flavor of acidic ingredients when recipes are made in quantity.

Original Recipe Yield

6 servings

Cooking Day

Mix oil, vinegar, garlic, salt, and pepper in small bowl. Transfer marinade to a large freezer bag. Add chicken to bag, turning to coat thoroughly. Freeze, using freezer bag method.

Serving Day

Thaw chicken completely. Place chicken, skin side up and well coated with marinade, into rimmed baking pan or dish. Roast uncovered in a 350 degree oven until brown and cooked through, about 35–40 minutes. Chicken may also be grilled over medium-hot coals until cooked through, turning once. Serve with salad, tomatoes, and cheese biscuits.

Serving Suggestion

If desired, you may substitute chicken breasts in this recipe. With breasts, you may also remove chicken from bone after cooking, slice, and use to top a salad. Make fresh marinade to use as salad dressing if desired.

Lighter Fare Nutritional Information (per serving): Calories 225.6; Total Fat 20.1g; Cholesterol 43.6mg; Sodium 47.7mg; Total Carbohydrates 1g; Fiber 0g; Protein 10.3g

Bangkok Chicken Satay

Chicken on a stick served with a peanut sauce

Contributed by Leslie Reisig—Castle Pines North, Colorado

	x3	x6	x9
1 lb. chicken breast, cut into 2 inch cubes	3 lbs	6 lbs	9 lbs
2 T. rice vinegar	¼c + 2T	¾c	1c + 2T
1 T. soy sauce	3T	¼c + 2T	½c + 1T
1 T. packed dark brown sugar	3T	¼c + 2T	½c + 1T
2 t. garlic, minced	2T	¼c	¼c + 2T
1 t. chopped fresh ginger	1T	2T	3T
¼ t. crushed red pepper flakes	¾t	1½t	2¼t

Serving Day

6 scallions, cut into 1 inch pieces
24 cherry tomatoes
skewers*

Peanut Sauce

1 T. peanut oil
½ cup onion, chopped
1 t. chopped fresh ginger
1 t. garlic, minced
½ cup creamy peanut butter
½ cup chicken broth
1 T. ketchup
2 T. rice vinegar
2 T. soy sauce
½ t. crushed red pepper flakes

*If you are using wooden skewers (for outdoor grilling), soak the skewers in water for at least 30 minutes before threading on the chicken and vegetables. This will keep the skewers from burning.

Original Recipe Yield

4 servings

Cooking Day

In a medium bowl, combine rice vinegar, soy sauce, brown sugar, garlic, ginger, and red pepper flakes. Place chicken in large freezer bag with marinade and freeze, using freezer bag method.

Serving Day

Peanut sauce: Heat peanut oil in skillet over medium heat, then add onion, ginger, and garlic; cook until onion is softened, about 4 minutes. Remove from heat and purée in blender or food processor with peanut butter, chicken broth, ketchup, rice vinegar, soy sauce, and pepper flakes until smooth. Sauce may be made up to one day ahead and stored in refrigerator until ready to use.

Thaw chicken completely. Remove chicken from marinade. Thread scallion pieces, tomatoes, and chicken onto skewers. Grill over medium heat, until chicken is tender and cooked through. Serve with peanut sauce for dipping.

Basil Grilled Tuna Kabobs

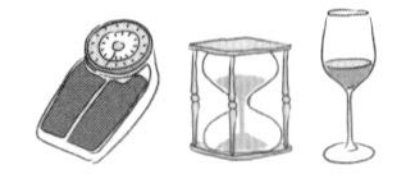

Fragrant and tender!

	x3	x6	x9
1½ lbs. fresh tuna steak, ¾–1 inch thick*	4½ lbs	9 lbs	13½ lbs
½ cup fresh basil, washed and stemmed	1½c	3c	4½c
3 cloves garlic, halved	9	18	27
3 strips lemon zest	9	18	27
¼ cup fresh lemon juice**	½c	1c	1½c
1 T. white wine vinegar**	2T	¼c	¼c + 2T
1 cup extra virgin olive oil	3c	6c	9c
1 t. kosher salt	1T	2T	3T
1 t. black pepper	1T	2T	3T

Serving Day

lemon or lime wedges and/or garlic butter sauce to drizzle over kabobs (optional)

grilled vegetables

*Use fresh tuna for freezing. Instead of cutting tuna into kabobs, whole tuna steaks may be used. Fresh swordfish or salmon may also be used for this recipe.

**This measurement, when multiplied, has been adjusted to accommodate the intensified flavor of acidic ingredients when recipes are made in quantity.

Original Recipe Yield

6–8 appetizers or 4–6 entrée servings

Cooking Day

Rinse tuna under cold water and blot dry with paper towels. (If tuna has dark or bloody spots, trim those off—they aren't harmful, just a little tough.) Cut the tuna into kabob-size pieces and place in a freezer bag. Refrigerate until marinade is completed.

For marinade: In a blender or food processor, combine basil, garlic, lemon zest, lemon juice, vinegar, oil, salt, and pepper. Purée until smooth. Pour over tuna, making sure that all surfaces of the tuna are covered. Seal bag and freeze, using freezer bag method.

Serving Day

Thaw tuna in refrigerator, allowing it to marinate. If you are using wooden skewers, soak the skewers in water for at least 30 minutes. Thread skewers with tuna. Spray grill surface with oil or cooking spray and grill tuna over medium-high heat until cooked to taste: 1–2 minutes per side for rare, 3–4 minutes per side for medium rare. The kabobs should be nicely browned on the outside. Test tuna for doneness. Rare will be soft to the touch; medium rare will have some resistance to the surface; medium will be quite firm. When cooking tuna medium well or well, lengthen cooking time in 1–2 minute increments, being careful not to overcook and dry out tuna. Serve kabobs with lemon or lime wedges, a light sprinkling of kosher salt, or garlic butter drizzle. These are also wonderful served with grilled vegetables.

Lighter Fare Nutritional Information (per serving): Calories 240; Total Fat 15g; Cholesterol 33mg; Sodium 220mg; Total Carbohydrates 1.6g; Dietary Fiber 0.2g; Protein 34.2g

Bombay Chicken Curry

A delicious and mild curry dish

	x3	x6	x9
½ cup butter, melted	1½c	3c	4½c
1 cup onion, diced	3c	6c	9c
1 clove garlic, minced	3	6	9
¼ cup flour	¾c	1½c	2¼c
2 T. curry powder	¼ c + 2T	¾c	1c + 2T
1 t. salt	1T	2T	3T
¼ t. pepper	¾t	1½t	2¼t
¼ t. ground ginger	¾t	1½t	2¼t
¼ t. cayenne pepper	¾t	1½t	2¼t
3 cups water	2qts + 1c	4qts + 2c	6qts + 3c
2 cups cooked chicken, chopped	6c	12c	18c

Original Recipe Yield

6 servings

Cooking Day

In a medium saucepan, sauté onion and garlic in butter. Add flour, curry powder, salt, pepper, ginger, and cayenne pepper. Continue cooking and stirring over medium heat until smooth. Add water and cooked chicken; simmer for 20–30 minutes, stirring occasionally, until sauce is bubbly and slightly thickened. Cool completely. Freeze, using freezer bag method.

Serving Day

Thaw chicken completely. Reheat over medium heat until heated through. Serve over rice with desired variety of toppings, such as mandarin oranges, banana slices, raisins, dry roasted peanuts, steamed snow peas, pineapple chunks, or flaked coconut.